Vilhelm Ludwig Peter Thomsen

The Relations Between Ancient Russia and Scandinavia

And the Origin of the Russian State

Vilhelm Ludwig Peter Thomsen

The Relations Between Ancient Russia and Scandinavia
And the Origin of the Russian State

ISBN/EAN: 9783337166434

Printed in Europe, USA, Canada, Australia, Japan

Cover: Foto ©Suzi / pixelio.de

More available books at **www.hansebooks.com**

THE RELATIONS

BETWEEN

ANCIENT RUSSIA AND SCANDINAVIA,

AND

THE ORIGIN OF THE RUSSIAN STATE.

THREE LECTURES

DELIVERED AT THE TAYLOR INSTITUTION, OXFORD,

IN MAY, 1876,

IN ACCORDANCE WITH THE TERMS

OF LORD ILCHESTER'S BEQUEST TO THE UNIVERSITY,

BY

DR. VILHELM THOMSEN,

Professor of Comparative Philology in the University of Copenhagen,
Member of the Royal Danish Academy of Sciences, &c.

. Oxford and London:

JAMES PARKER AND CO.

1877.

OXFORD:

By E. Pickard Hall, M.A., and J. H. Stacy,

PRINTERS TO THE UNIVERSITY.

PREFACE.

THE Lectures which are here presented to the public were delivered at Oxford in May, 1876, by invitation of the Curators of the Taylor Institution as administrators of the Ilchester Bequest for the encouragement of the study of the Slavonic Language, Literature, and History. Within the boundaries set by the terms of the endowment, it was natural to me to choose a subject which, at the same time as being Slavonic, had some reference to Scandinavia, and I could not long be in doubt as to the choice.

I give the Lectures here, in the main, so as I had at first written them, with such slight modifications and additions as, in revising my manuscript, I thought necessary. According to this plan I have not hesitated to insert several details of a philological kind which I was obliged to leave out or abridge when delivering the Lectures, but which are in fact so important to the purpose I had set myself that it seemed to me they could not well be omitted here; such will be found, for instance, in the inquiry into the names of the Dnieper rapids, the Old Russian proper names, the history of the name Varangian, &c.

I hope that the book may have gained by this, and I shall be glad if I have succeeded in contributing somewhat towards the final and impartial solution of a historic-ethnographical problem which may possibly have some interest also to English readers.

I beg to express my best thanks first and foremost to the Curators of the Taylor Institution, not only for their honourable invitation to lecture at Oxford, but also for their liberality in undertaking the printing of the Lectures at the cost of the endowment; next, to all those who have met me with kindness, as well with respect to the present work, as during my stay in England. Among them I must be allowed to offer my special thanks to one of the Curators, the Rev. G. W. Kitchin, who has also kindly assisted me in reading the proofs, an assistance all the more valuable in that it has been afforded to one who is writing in a foreign language.

COPENHAGEN,
November, 1877.

CONTENTS.

LECTURE I.

FROM the first dawn of authentic history that vast
territory which now constitutes European Russia, or at
least the large central portion of it, appears to have
been inhabited, in the main, by the same nationalities
which still form the bulk of its population, that is,
partly by Slavonians, partly by Finnish and Tataric
tribes. But the relations between these various nationalities were then quite different from what they are
at the present day; the overwhelming superiority,
numerically and politically speaking, which the Slavonic element has acquired over the others, has been
the work of comparatively modern times, while the
foundation of a Russian state belongs to none of
them.

We must for a moment glance at the primitive
history of the Slavonians in Russia and the ethnography of that extensive country at the period when
we first meet with the name of Russia.

The Slavs or Slavonians are a branch of that great
family which we call the Aryan or the Indo-European
family, which, from time out of mind, has occupied by
far the greater part of Europe. Of course the Slavonians have lived in our part of the world quite as

B

long as any of their brother-peoples ; but, except their
very nearest kinsmen and neighbours, the Lithuanians
and the Lets, there are none of the Aryan tribes upon
which history begins to cast its light so late as upon
the Slavonians. Their domicile was so remote from
the centres of ancient culture, that the Greeks and
Romans could scarcely come into direct contact with
them ; and having always been, as they are still, by
nature a peaceable people, they themselves never
greatly interfered in the affairs of their border-lands.
This is the reason why the Slavonians were so late
in making their appearance on the stage of history.

It was only when the Romans had already got
footing in Germany, that they became aware, through
the Germans, of the existence of the Slavonians, and
that we begin to find them mentioned by classic
authors. The first Latin author who clearly alludes
to them is Pliny the elder (+ 79 A.D.); and he ex-
presses himself very cautiously thus : 'Some say the
countries beyond the Vistula are inhabited by the
Sarmates, the *Venedi*[1],' &c. A little later we again
find the *Veneti* mentioned by the Roman historian
Tacitus in his description of Germany (ch. xlvi); he
is in doubt whether this people is to be numbered
among the Germans or not ; however, he is inclined
to believe that they should be so, because they greatly
resemble the Germans in their mode of living. . From
this time the name of the Slavonians appears a little
more frequently in the historical and geographical
works of antiquity.

---

[1] Pliny, Hist. Natur. iv. § 96 (14): 'Quidam haec habitari ad Vis-
tulam usque fluvium a Sarmatis, Venedis, Sciris, Hirris tradunt.'

The name under which the Slavonians appear in ancient literature, is generally *Venedi* or *Veneti* (*Venadi, Vinidae,* Οὐενέδαι). This name, unknown to the Slavonians themselves, is that by which the Teutonic tribes have from the first designated these their eastern neighbours, viz. *Wends,* and the use of this appellation by the Roman authors plainly shows that their knowledge of the Slavonians was derived only from the Germans. The Old German form of this name was *Winedâ,* and *Wenden* is the name which the Germans of the present day give to the remnants of a Slavonic population, formerly large, who now inhabit Lusatia, while they give the name of *Winden* to the Slovens in Carinthia, Carniola, and Styria; we find the Anglo-Saxon form, *Winedas, Weonodas,* in King Alfred's Orosius, as a designation of the Wends or Slavonians south of the Baltic, and *Vender* (in the Old Norse *Vindr*) was the name under which this wild heathen people was known in the North, especially in Denmark, during the middle ages (11th and 12th centuries). Also the Finnish nations that border the Baltic and the gulf of Bothnia in ancient time borrowed this name from the Scandinavians or the Goths, and still apply it to Russia, which is called by the Finlanders *Venäjä, Venää,* or *Venät,* and by the Esthonians *Vene*[1]. If the Slavonians themselves ever applied any common name to the whole of their family, it must most probably have been that by which we now are accustomed to call them, *Slavs,* or *Slavonians;* its original

---

[1] Comp. V. Thomsen, Den gotiske Sprogklasses Indflydelse på den finske, Kübenhavn, 1869, p. 109, 159.

native form was *Slovêne.* Usually, however, each of
the numerous tribes into which the Slavonians were
divided from days of yore called itself by some
peculiar name, and even the name *Slovêne* never
appears as a common appellation, handed down by
tradition, but only as a name which different tribes
far remote from each other applied to themselves.

The most ancient sources from which we derive a
knowledge of the Wends or Slavonians, unanimously
place them by the Vistula. From that river, which
must have formed their western frontier, they extended eastward to the Dnieper, and even beyond.
To the south the Carpathians formed their boundary.
To the north they perhaps crossed the Dwina into
the territory afterwards known as Novgorod.

In the extensive woods and marshes which cover
these remote tracts the Slavonians seem to have
dwelt in peace and quiet during the first centuries
after Christ, divided into a number of small tribes or
clans, providing for their own wants without troubling
their neighbours, if they themselves were not molested,
and almost uninfluenced by the events which in
those times disturbed the greater part of Europe.
At any rate, history has handed nothing down to us
which can lead us to suppose that the Slavs had, at
that period, taken part in those important events.

In the third or fourth century the Goths advanced
from the southern shores of the Baltic, through the
western part of what now constitutes Russia. One
of their leaders, the conqueror Ermanarik, having
established here for a short time a powerful kingdom,
the Slavs also were compelled to bow beneath his

yoke. But the Goths soon moved off southwards, and their relations to the Slavs of Russia were at an end.

I must not here omit to refer to an interesting little discovery lately made, which, in my opinion, must certainly have come down to us from these Gothic immigrants. It consists of a spear-head bearing a short Runic inscription, which has been found in the neighbourhood of a town called Kovel in Volhynia. This inscription is in the so-called ancient runes, and the period to which it must belong is thus clearly determined as the third or fourth century A.D. It consists only of a man's name—no doubt the owner's—which from the characters must probably be read E(r̃)LARIDS[1]. The period and the idiomatic form of the inscribed name make it almost impossible not to see in it a memento of the invasion of these lands by the Goths.

It was not long, however, before their primitive home became too narrow for the Slavs, and as their numbers could no longer be contained within their ancient boundaries—and, perhaps, compelled to it by pressure from without—they began to spread themselves to the west, in which direction the great

---

[1] This discovery has just now been made public by A. Szumowski, together with a letter on the Runic inscription written by the Danish runologist, Dr. L. Wimmer, in the Polish Review, Wiadomości Archeologiczne, vol. iii. p. 49-61. Warsaw, 1876. The spear-head itself has, both in workmanship and ornamentation, an extraordinary resemblance to one found near Müncheberg in the province of Brandenburg, which is represented in Professor G. Stephens's Old Northern Runic Monuments, vol. ii. p. 880.

migrations of the fourth and fifth centuries had made abundant room for the new immigrants.

By two different roads the Slavs now begin to advance in great masses. On the one side, they cross the Vistula and extend over the tracts between the Carpathian mountains and the Baltic, right down to the Elbe, the former Germanic | population of this region having either emigrated or being exhausted by their intestine contests and their deadly struggle with the Roman empire. By this same road the *Poles,* and probably also the *Chekhs* of Bohemia and Moravia, reached the districts they have inhabited since that period. In the rest of this western territory the Slavonians were afterwards almost exterminated during their bloody wars with the Germans, so that but few of their descendants exist.

The other road by which the Slavonians advanced lay to the south-west, along the course of the Danube. These are the so-called South-Slavonians: the *Bulgarians,* the *Servians,* the *Croatians,* and farthest westward, the *Slovens.* A thousand years ago, however, the Slavonians occupied in this their new home a still more extensive tract of land than they do now ; in the south Slavonic colonies were to be found far down the Græco-Turkish peninsula, and northward their territory extended over a large portion of what was anciently Dacia and Pannonia, — the country which, a little later, the Hungarians made their home.

These Southern Slavs have played an important part with regard to the whole race, inasmuch as they have been the intermediate link between Christian-

ized civilisation and their own heathen kindred
tribes. It was to the Danubian Slavs (especially
in Pannonia) that the two Thessalonian brothers,
Cyrillus and Methodius, the national saints of the
Slavonians, preached the gospel in their (Bulgarian?)
mother-tongue in the latter part of the ninth century,
and founded a flourishing literature. By the spread
of Christianity to the other Southern and Eastern
Slavs, this literature found a new home, and until a
few centuries ago, this ' *Old Slavonic* ' tongue, in a
slightly modified form, was the only written language
of these nations. Even at the present day it is the
language used by the Greek Church in their religious
services.

Of the Slavonians who remained in their ancient
home, which now forms the western part of Russia,
we hear little or nothing for several centuries. The
first document which gives us an explicit account of
them is the old Russian chronicle, which bears the
name of the monk Nestor ($+$ c. 1115?): in this work
the father of Russian history has bequeathed us an
extremely valuable sketch of the ancient history of
his native land to about the year 1110. The author
begins his work with a description of the Slavonic
tribes who dwelt in what is now called Russia at the
commencement of Russian history, that is to say, in
the ninth century, and we perceive that the Slavs at
that period were just as far from forming a nation as
they were when we first found them mentioned in
history; they were divided into a number of tribes,
each independent of the other, and each enjoying but
little order in its internal social state.

These tribes were, according to Nestor, the *Slovêne* (or Slavonians κατ᾽ ἐξοχήν) round Lake Ilmen, with Novgorod for their capital; to the south of them lay the *Krivichi* round the sources of the Volga, the Dwina, and the Dnieper, with Smolensk for their capital; west of them was a kindred tribe, the *Polochane*, by the little river Polota and the Dwina, their capital being Polotsk. In the tract of land lying to the west of the Dnieper we find, if we turn southwards, first the *Dregovichi*, then the *Drevliane*, and farther on the *Poliane*, one of the most important of them all, whose capital, Kiev, became so celebrated in later times; besides some tribes of less importance. On the eastern side of the Dnieper we meet with a few Slavonic tribes, namely, the *Radimichi*, south of Smolensk, the *Viatichi* near Oka, the most easterly of all the tribes, and lastly the *Severiane*, just opposite the *Poliane*.

You will perceive that even at this time a single tribe only, the Viatichi, had reached the centre of what is now called Russia; the Slavs cannot have established themselves much farther east than they had done four hundred years before, when these districts were the common home of the whole race. I must further call your attention to the fact that the name *Russians* was still completely unknown, and as yet applied to none of the Slavonic tribes mentioned by Nestor.

If we cast a glance beyond the boundaries of the Slavonic world, we find the greater part of what is now called Russia peopled by Finnish and Tataric tribes. The broad belt of steppes which covers the southern part of that country, and which in antiquity had been inhabited principally by the Scyths, was at that time occupied by hordes of Tatar or Turkish origin, living more or less as nomads. The *Khazars* were the most important of these tribes at the opening of Russian history. In the latter half of the seventh century A.D. they had formed a state, the capital of which was *Itil* on the Volga, in the neighbourhood of the modern town of Astrachan. A fortress of theirs is also mentioned, *Sarkel,* ' the White House,' constructed with the assistance of Greek engineers about 835, probably on the lower course of the river Don. By degrees the greater part of what is now southern Russia fell into their power, and in the ninth century the Slavonic tribes nearest to their frontier, the Polians, the Severians and the Viatichi, were forced to become their tributaries. The state of the Khazarian 'Khagan,' as their prince was titled, won the respect even of the Greeks, and the extensive trade carried on by his subjects made them frequent guests in Constantinople. It was reserved to the Russian princes by degrees to repel the Khazars, till, in the year 969, their power was finally crushed by the conquest and destruction of their capital Itil, their fortress Sarkel having been taken four years earlier by the Russian prince Sviatoslav.

North of the Khazars, along the Volga, particularly on the left bank of that river, dwelt several other Tatar tribes. The most important of these were the *Bulgarians* of the Volga and the Kama. This people is very frequently mentioned by historians, and we learn that they were not nomads, like so many of their kindred tribes, but had fixed dwelling-places. They employed themselves in agriculture, and also in trade, which indeed was their chief occupation, and their capital, *Bulgar*, near the modern town of Kazan, was frequented by numerous merchants who reached it by the Volga. Between the territory occupied by Slavs and the Volga, as well as throughout the whole of the northern part of the extensive Russian dominions, dwelt a number of Finnish tribes, of which many exist at the present day, though they are now more or less intermingled with the Russians, and are certainly not so numerous as in former times. Thus Nestor mentions the *Mordvins* (*Mordva*), the most southern tribe of all, now settled between the Oka and the Volga. To the north of them, in the present governments of Viatka and Kazan, we still find the *Cheremis*, *Cheremisa* of Nestor. If we turn to the north-west, we find north of the Slavonians of Novgorod, dwelling round the Gulf of Finland and Lake Ladoga, different Finnish tribes, nearly akin to the inhabitants of Finland, whom the Russian chronicles comprise under the common name *Chud'*. These, with the Lettish and Lithuanian tribes who dwelt to the south of them, west of the Krivichi and the Polochans, completely excluded the Slavs from the Baltic and its bays.

The tribes whom Nestor mentions as dwelling nearest to the Slavs on their eastern side, in the centre of modern Russia, have, on the contrary, quite disappeared, having been gradually absorbed by the Slavonian nationality. He thus names one tribe, *Muroma*, who lived near the Oka, to the north-west

of the Mordvins, and who probably were nearly akin
to them. This tribe has long ago become extinct.
Its name however still exists as the name of an
ancient town, Murom, on the Oka. To the north of
them dwelt the *Meria*, and farther northward the
Ves', two tribes which once were doubtless large and
important. Jordanes, in his History of the Goths,
names the *Vasina* (?), the *Merens*, and the *Mordens*
(i. e. the Ves, the Meria, and the Mordvins), among
the peoples who had once been subjugated by the
Gothic conqueror Ermanarik. The name of the Ves
occurs too in Arabic authors as *Visu*. According to
Nestor the two lakes, Rostov and Kleshtchino (or
Pereyaslavl), formed the centre of the Merian territory, while the Ves are said to have dwelt near the
lake Bielo-ozero.

Of the extinct Finnish tribes the Meria is perhaps
the one of which we know the most. From 1851 to
1854 a Russian archæologist, Count A. Uvarov, with
great energy undertook a long series of researches in
the territory the Merians inhabited in former times.
In the course of his enquiry he opened no less than
7729 barrows, of which in this district there is an
immense number, often, as it were, massed together as
in great cemeteries. His researches have brought to
light a great many antiquities of all kinds,—weapons
(axes and spears, but no swords, this weapon being
unknown to all Finnish tribes), household utensils,
furniture, ornaments, coins, &c. &c., which had been
buried with the deceased. These antiquities, which
are now deposited in a museum in Moscow, cast a
new light on the manners and customs of this tribe,

long since extinct[1]. The insight we have thus acquired enables us to judge of the mode of living, &c.,
of their kindred tribes of whom no such relics exist.
It is needless here to particularise these results, which
are not connected with our subject. I will only
remark that it must have been a barbarous tribe
and but little civilised, chiefly engaged in war and
the chase. The discovery of numerous coins, Arabic
and of the west of Europe, indicates that they carried
on commerce, and also proves that their nationality
and their peculiar customs were still in existence
in the twelfth century, for the most modern coins
which have been found belong to that age. But
from that time their denationalisation must have
advanced with rapid strides, contemporaneously with
the spread of Christianity and the immigration of
Slavonic settlers.

It is not necessary to dwell any longer on the list
of names of other tribes ; these few remarks must
suffice to give a general idea of the ethnographic
relations that existed in the ninth century in the
lands now known to us as Russia. We find that
extensive country peopled by a number of tribes
of different descent—Slavs, Finns, Tatars—united
by no common tie and all generally but little civilised. It was only about the middle of the ninth
century that the foundation was laid of the *Russian*
state, the first nucleus of that mighty empire which

---

[1] Comp. Étude sur les peuples primitifs de la Russie. Les Mériens.
Par le Comte A. Ouvaroff. Trad. du Russe par M. F. Malaqué.
St. Pétb. 1875.

has afterwards united all these various races into one political body.

'In the year 859,' says Nestor[1], 'came the Varangians from beyond the sea and demanded tribute from the Chud and from the Slavonians, the Meria, the Ves and the Krivichi; but the Khazars took tribute of the Polians, the Severians, and of the Viatichi.'

Then he continues : 'In the year 862 they drove the Varangians over the sea, and paid them no tribute, and they began to govern themselves, and there was no justice among them, and clan rose against clan, and there was internal strife between them, and they began to make war upon each other. And they said to each other : Let us seek for a prince who can reign over us and judge what is right. And they went over the sea to the Varangians, to *Rus'*, for so were these Varangians called : they were called *Rus'* as others are called *Svie* (Swedes), others *Nurmane* (Northmen, Norwegians), others *Angliane* (English, or Angles of Sleswick?), others *Gote* (probably the inhabitants of the island of Gothland). The Chud, the Slavonians, the Krivichi and the Ves said to Rus : Our land is large and rich, but there is no order in it; come ye and rule and reign over us. And three brothers were chosen with their whole clan, and they took with them all the Rus, and they came. And the eldest, Rurik, settled in Novgorod[2],

---

[1] Chronica Nestoris edidit Fr. Miklosich, p. 9–10. Vindobonae, 1860. Лѣтопись по Лаврентіевскому списку. Изданіе археографической коммиссіи, стр. 18–19. Санктпетерб., 1872.

[2] According to several manuscripts (e.g. the Hypatian and the Radzi-

and the second, Sineus, near Bielo-ozero, and the third, Truvor, in Izborsk.   And the Russian land, Novgorod, was called after these Varangians; they are the Novgorodians of Varangian descent; previously the Novgorodians were Slavonians.   But after the lapse of two years Sineus and his brother Truvor died, and Rurik assumed the government and divided the towns among his men, to one Polotsk, to another Rostov, to another Bielo-ozero.'

Such is Nestor's naïve description of the foundation of the Russian state.   If it be read without prejudice or sophistical comment, it cannot be doubted that the word *Varangians* is used here as a common term for the inhabitants of Scandinavia, and that *Rus'* was meant to be the name of a particular Scandinavian tribe; this tribe, headed by Rurik and his brothers, is said to have crossed the sea and founded a state whose capital, for a time, was Novgorod, and this state was the nucleus of the present Russian empire.

Next, Nestor tells us that in the same year two of Rurik's men, 'who were not of his family,' Askold and Dir, separated themselves from him with the intention to go to Constantinople.   They went down the Dnieper; but when they arrived at Kiev, the capital of the Polians, who at that time were tributary to the Khazars, they preferred to stay there, and

---

will MSS.) Rurik first settles in Ladoga (upon river Volkhov, near its outlet into Lake Ladoga), and only after the death of his brothers moves to Novgorod. See Лѣтопись по Ипатіевскому списку. Изданіе археографической коммиссіи, стр. 11. Санктпетербо., 1871. Bielowski, Monumenta Poloniae historica, vol. i. p. 564. Lemberg, 1864.   A. L. Schlözer, Несторъ, Russische Annalen, vol. i. p. 188 ff. Göttingen, 1802.

founded in that town an independent principality. Twenty years after, in 882, this principality was incorporated by Rurik's successor Oleg : by a stratagem he made himself master of the town and killed Askold and Dir, and from this time Kiev, 'the mother of all Russian towns,' as it was called, remained the capital of the Russian state and the centre of the Russian name.

Some details of minor importance in Nestor's account may be doubtful or need a critical sifting ; in the third lecture I shall return to this question. But this circumstance does not influence the chief point, the express statement that the tribe that founded the Russian state and gave it its name, was of Scandinavian origin. For this tribe I will use in the sequel the name *Russ*, to distinguish them from the modern Slavonic *Russians*.

It is true that in many cases it is a difficult task for critics to re-establish the original wording of the so-called Nestorian text, in consequence of the peculiar manner in which the Russian chronicles have come down to us: each transcriber having at pleasure altered or added to the wording of the text, and the oldest manuscripts we possess not being of earlier date than the fourteenth century. But the statement of the chronicles as to the origin of the Russian state is one of the invariable points in them. It is not only common to all copies, but it runs like a red thread through the whole of the ancient history of Russia, and it must therefore have belonged even to the archetype itself of the chronicle, as it was penned at the beginning of the twelfth century. To suppose that in the course of little more than two hundred years the tradition could have been falsified to such a degree, that the oldest chroniclers could have been completely mistaken, is absurd/ Conjecture

From the time historical critics first became acquainted with Nestor's account, that is to say from the beginning of the last century, until about fifteen or twenty years ago, scarcely any one ventured to doubt the accuracy of his statement. Plenty of evidence was even gradually produced from other sources to corroborate in the most striking manner the tradition of the Russian chronicles. A few voices, it is true, had been raised against it, and had advocated different views. Thus Ewers, a German savant[1], was pleased to turn the Varangians, who founded the Russian state, into Khazars, while several Slavonic scholars regarded them as Slavs from Prussia or Holsatia. But all their arguments were easily confuted and found but little credence. The descent of the ancient Russ from the Scandinavians seemed to be irrefutably established to the satisfaction of all sober students both Russian and foreign, especially since the Russian historian, M. Pogodin, whose death last year (1875) science has to lament, warmly defended it in a number of writings in his native tongue[2], and E. Kunik, Member of the Academy of St. Petersburg, with profound learning

---

[1] In his work Ursprung des Russischen Staats. Riga and Leipzig, 1808.

[2] E. g. O происхожденіи Руси (i.e. On the Origin of the Russ), Moscow, 1825. Изслѣдованія, замѣчанія и лекціи о древней русской исторіи (i.e. Researches, Remarks and Lectures on Ancient Russian History), vol. i–iii. ibid. 1846 ff.

Critics of the theory

had explained the philological side of the question in
his important work entitled, 'Die Berufung der schwedischen Rodsen durch die Finnen und Slawen,' 2 vols,
(St. Petersburg, 1844–45.)

In Russia itself, however, there was a party which
still shrank from acknowledging the foreign origin
of the Russian name by accepting this theory;
and in 1859 a storm was raised against the so-called
Northman or Scandinavian school. The attack was
opened by V. Lamanski in a Russian work entitled
'On the Slavs of Asia Minor, Africa, and Spain,'
in which the author advocated the Slavonic origin
of the Russ; and in the following year (1860) a
work was published by N. I. Kostomarov, 'On the
Origin of Russia' (О началѣ Руси), which attempted
to prove that the Varangians, who were called in
by the Slavs and Finns in 862, were Lithuanians.
Since that time a complete deluge of works and
pamphlets have appeared in Russia, all intended to
weaken the authority of the venerable Nestor, and
to combat the arguments of the Scandinavian school[1].
That is really the only point on which the different
authors are agreed. For the rest they differ materially
in their opinions; most of them, however, advocate
the Slavonic origin of the Russ, and, in direct contradiction to the unanimous testimony of all records,
assume that they had always lived in southern
Russia[2].

It would be wearisome to dwell longer on the

[1] A list of this literature is given by Kunik in Mémoires de l'Académie
Impériale de St. Pétersbourg, vii. série, t. xxiii. pp. 279 ff., 409 ff.
[2] Comp. e.g. the Athenæum, July 27, 1872, p. 113 ff.

C

details of this literature. It is really but a slight
portion of it that has any scientific value. I shall
only name one author of this school whose work bears
at least the impress of serious thought and much
learning; I mean S. Gedeonov, who has written
'Researches on the Varangian Question [1].' By far
the greater part of these writings are of such
a nature as to possess no claim to be called
scientific: any really scientific method is superseded
by the vaguest and most arbitrary fancies, which
appear to be inspired more by ill-judged national
fanaticism than by serious desire to discover the truth.
Every impartial reader must receive the impression
that their only aim is, at any cost, to suppress the
unpleasant fact that the origin of the Russian state
was due to a foreign race of princes—as if such a
circumstance could in any way be dishonouring to a
great nation.

The new theories, here alluded to, have not failed
to find contradiction even in Russia itself. The old
champions, Pogodin and especially Kunik, have re-
peatedly entered the lists in defence of their favourite
subject, and in one work after another have combated
the vague fancies of their adversaries, and other
scholars, not less temperate than the first mentioned,
have intrepidly followed their example. It has certainly been acknowledged that the criticism of the
anti-Scandinavianists has cast a new light upon some
details of the question. But the chief question is
quite uninfluenced hereby, and, generally speaking,

_____

[1] Изслѣдованія о Варяжскомъ вопросѣ, printed as appendices to
Записки Импер. Академіи наукъ. i–iii. St. Petersburg, 1862.

the theory of the Scandinavian origin of the Russ has not yet been shaken a hair's breadth.

However, it cannot be wondered that people who are not able themselves to judge the question profoundly and impartially may have received another impression from its discussion. Thus anti-Scandinavianism appears to have become almost an article of faith with Russian patriots, and has even found its way, as an incontestable fact, to certain class-books of Russian history. On the other side, the great number of discrepant opinions that have been put forth, in the eyes of many persons, have rendered the question so obscure and intricate that they begin to doubt the possibility of its being cleared up. Even so impartial a scholar as R. G. Latham[1] has not been able to come to a satisfactory solution, but in a very singular manner, that can be explained only by an imperfect knowledge of the details of the question, hesitates between different views, taking his exceptions to all of them. However he seems most inclined to regard the stock of the Russ as Goths, a view involving a confusion which cannot be sufficiently deprecated.

Under these circumstances it is certainly time that the question of the origin of the Russ should be subjected to a fresh discussion carried on according to the method of modern science, and that Scandinavian philologists especially should contribute to its solution. This is the task I have set myself in these lectures. I hope to be able to treat this subject without laying myself open to the accusation of undue partiality and

[1] The Nationalities of Europe, vol. i. p. 364 ff. London, 1863.

national prejudice, and to prove to your satisfaction
that the tribe which in the ninth century founded the
Russian state, and to whom the name Russ was
originally applied, really were 'Northmen' or Scandinavians of Swedish origin.

This is not only the explicit tradition in Russia
itself, handed down to us by the chronicles in the
most clear and incontestable language, but it is also
corroborated, directly or indirectly, by abundance of
evidence from other sources, linguistic, historical, and
archæological.

There are two literatures especially which have
preserved most valuable notices respecting the Russ,
and which therefore, together with the native chronicles, furnish us with the most important information
with reference to our subject, viz. the literature of
the Byzantine empire and that of Arabia.

From their first appearance in Russia the Russ
carried on a lively intercourse with Greece [1]. The
name by which the Greeks mention them is *Rhôs*
('Ρῶς) or *Rusioi* ('Ρούσιοι); this latter form however
does not occur before the middle of the tenth century;
till then the form 'Ρῶς is exclusively used. The first
time we meet with this name is in the year 839, in a
passage which I shall review in my next lecture.
There is really no suggestion which would lead us to
suppose that the Greeks before that time had come
into contact with the people they called *Rhôs;* their
closer relation to them is even considerably later,

---

[1] Comp. Rambaud, L'Empire Grec au dixième siècle, p. 364 ff.
Paris, 1870. Gibbon, The History of the Decline and Fall of the
Roman Empire, ch. lv. 3.

a fact which highly corroborates the approximate correctness, at least, of Nestor's chronology.

The anti-Scandinavianists have sought to prove that Greek documents recognise the existence of the Russ long before that time. Because they think they have proved Nestor untrustworthy with respect to his chronology, they conclude that his statement in general is a mere fiction. But apart from the injustice of such a conclusion, the proofs adduced are completely untenable. I will venture to speak of a passage of which much has been made. It is from a Greek author, Theophanes Isaakios (+817). He relates that the Greek emperor Constantine Copronymos, in the year 773, made war on the Bulgarians who dwelt near the Danube. He first dispatched a great army in 2000 galleys, and then himself sailed off on board some other galleys which are called τὰ ῥούσια χελάνδια[1]. These ῥούσια χελάνδια have been interpreted as 'the Russian galleys.' But we must observe that the word ῥούσιος in the signification of *Russian* is not to be found in Greek before the middle of the tenth century. Until that period those people were always called 'Ῥῶς, and the adjective formed from that word was ῥωσικός; in the next place it is expressly said that the Russ did not use 'chelandia,' which were a very large kind of ship, but that they always used small ships or boats[2]. The fact is simply this,

---

[1] Τούτῳ τῷ ἔτει μηνὶ Μαΐῳ ἰνδικτιῶνος ιβ' ἐκίνησε Κωνσταντῖνος στόλον χελανδίων δισχιλ'ων κατὰ Βουλγαρίας, καὶ εἰσελθὼν καὶ αὐτὸς εἰς τὰ ῥούσια χελάνδια ἀπεκίνησε πρὸς τὸ ἐλθεῖν εἰς τὸν Δανούβιον ποταμόν. Theophanis Chronographia, ex recensione Jo. Classeni, vol. i. p. 691. Bonnae, 1839.

[2] 'Rusorum etenim naves ob parvitatem sui, ubi aquae minimum

ῥούσιος is a common Greek word signifying *red*. We
learn elsewhere that at that period the ships in which
the Greek emperor sailed were painted red[1]; and
the expression τὰ ῥούσια χελάνδια has nothing at all
to do with the Russ, but only means 'the red (or
imperial) galleys,' in opposition to the common war
(or transport) galleys in which the army sailed[2].
Consequently this argument proves nothing[3]. It is
incontestable that the first time the Greeks came in
contact with the Russ, as far as we know, was in 838
or 839, and this is also the only time the name Russ
is mentioned in any document before the time of
Rurik[4].

But nearly thirty years elapsed before the Greeks,
to their sorrow, made a closer acquaintance with this
tribe of bold and bloodthirsty warriors. The Russ
had scarcely got a footing on the banks of lake Ilmen

---

est, transeunt, quod Grecorum chelándia ob profunditatem sui facere
nequeunt.' Liudprand, Antapodosis, lib. v. c. 15 (Pertz, Monumenta
Germaniae histor., Scriptores, vol. iii. p. 331).

[1] Εἰs ῥούσιον ἀγράριον εἰσήρχετο., Constantine Porphyrog., de administrando Imperio, c. 51.

[2] The Roman Anastasius also, who in the latter half of the ninth century translated the Chronography of Theophanes into Latin (Historia
ecclesiastica ex Theophane), and who had himself sojourned at Constantinople, renders thus the passage in question: ' et ingressus ipse in rubea
chelandia motus est ad intrandum Danubium amnem' (Theophanis
Chronographia, vol. ii. p. 243. Bonnac, 1841).

[3] Comp. Kunik in Mémoires de l'Académie Imp. des sciences de
St. Pétersbourg, viie série, tom. xxiii. p. 222 ff. Some other supposed
proofs of a similar kind, but still feebler, have been, as it seems to me,
completely refuted by Kunik, particularly in his treatise O записк
готскаго топарха, in Записки имп. Академіи наукъ. vol. xxiv. 1874.

[4] Comp. Rambaud, L'Empire Grec au dixième siècle, pp. 371,
372.

and the Dnieper, before the contiguous native tribes
felt the might of these conquering invaders; and
the splendour and wealth of Constantinople itself, the
brilliant capital of the Oriental world, the heiress of
Roman power and civilisation, soon attracted their
greedy eyes, and for some time made the imperial
city the longed-for goal of their expeditions.

In 865 the Russ started from Kiev, then ruled by
Askold and Dir, went down the Dnieper, crossed the
Black Sea, and having in the most cruel manner
ravaged with fire and sword the coasts and isles
of the Black Sea and the Propontis, suddenly appeared with a fleet of 200 vessels before the peaceful
and unsuspecting capital which hitherto had at most
held friendly intercourse with them, and only by
rumour knew of their raids upon the neighbouring
tribes. The consternation in the city was general.
Nobody seems to have thought of defence, but with
the emperor and the patriarch Photios at their head,
the inhabitants had recourse to ceremonies and prayers
to the Holy Virgin. And really the town was saved
as it were by a miracle. A storm suddenly arose
which destroyed the vessels of the heathen Russ, so
that only a few of them escaped the general destruction. It is rather an interesting fact, that besides the
accounts of the chronicles on this expedition, two
direct documents concerning it have been preserved.
A few years ago two sermons of the patriarch Photios,
entitled ' On the occasion of the attack of the Rhos '
(εἰς τὸν ἔφοδον τῶν 'Ρῶς), were discovered in Russia;
and an encyclical epistle from him to the Oriental
bishops, written at the end of 866 with especial

reference to the same event, is in existence. In this
epistle he mentions the people called Rhos, which
(to use his own words) 'has often been spoken of by
many, a people which surpasses all others in ferocity
and bloodthirstiness. After having subdued the nations surrounding them, these Rhos have now carried
their overweening pride so far as to raise their hands
even against the Roman empire[1].' He adds, 'even
these people have now left their heathen and ungodly
religion, and are converted to Christianity, and they
have received a bishop;' however, there is every
reason for doubting whether this conversion was of
any extent or durability[2].

The next expedition of the Russ was undertaken
in 907 by Oleg, at the head of a fleet of 2000 vessels,
and was crowned with more success. This time too
they ravaged in the most cruel manner the coasts and
suburbs of Constantinople, but the Greeks having
barricaded the entrance to the city from the sea-side
the Russ could not force their way into it, until,
according to the relation of Nestor, who is our only authority for this expedition, Oleg had his ships dragged
on shore and put on wheels; the wind filled the sails,
and in this way they sailed on dry land towards the
town. Confounded by the strange sight, the Greeks
sent to Oleg, offering to pay him whatever tribute he

---

[1] Τὸ παρὰ πολλοῖς πολλάκις θρυλλούμενον (ἔθνος) καὶ εἰς ὠμότητα καὶ
μιαιφονίαν πάντας δευτέρους ταττόμενον, τοῦτο δὴ τὸ καλούμενον τὸ 'Ρῶς,
οἱ δὴ καὶ κατὰ τῆς 'Ρωμαϊκῆς ἀρχῆς, τοὺς πέριξ αὐτῶν δουλωσάμενοι,
κἀκεῖθεν ὑπέρογκα φρονηματισθέντες, χεῖρας ἀντῆραν. Photii Epistolae
ed. Richard. Montacutius, p. 58. Londini, 1651.

[2] Comp. Rambaud, L'Empire Grec au dixième siècle, p. 382 ff.

might demand. The Greeks were then obliged to disburse an enormous ransom, and to consent to a peace very advantageous to the Russ. Five years later the conditions of this peace were more exactly stipulated in a mutual treaty, the wording of which is handed down to us by Nestor.

The successor of Oleg was Igor, who in his turn undertook against the Greek empire two expeditions, of which several documents give us a description. The first took place in 941, and was particularly directed against the Asiatic coasts of the Black Sea. But it ended very unfortunately. The imperial army fell upon Igor, and the famous Greek fire especially caused dreadful destruction to his vessels, and spread panic among his people, of whom but a remnant returned home to tell their countrymen the issue of the expedition.

Thirsting for revenge, Igor assembled an enormous army, comprising both his subjects and hired troops, and in 944 again appeared off the Greek coasts with a numerous fleet; this time he won an easy victory. As soon as the Greeks had notice of the approach of the Russian army, they humbled themselves again and purchased for an enormous sum a peace, which, in the following year, was confirmed by a new treaty.

During the succeeding hundred years some other expeditions were undertaken by the Russ against the Greek empire, but with little success; after 1043 those attacks of the Russ cease altogether.

It was not, however, merely as pirates and warriors that the Russ came into contact with the Greeks.

What attracted them to Constantinople, far more than the uncertain chance of booty and tribute, was trade[1]. At the beginning of every summer great fleets of Russian merchantmen regularly arrived at the Greek capital. The wares they brought with them were chiefly the furs of all kinds which they had obtained from the tribes subject to them; also slaves, honey, &c.; in return Greece provided them with articles of luxury, ornaments of gold and silver, silk and other costly stuffs, specially what is called in Slavonic *pavolok*, in Old Norse *pell*, probably a kind of brocade; they also took the wines and the fruits of the South, &c. Of the extent and importance of this commerce we have plenty of proofs from different sources; I shall presently give an analysis of a very interesting passage upon this subject from an illustrious Greek author, the emperor Constantine Porphyrogenitus himself. The two treaties between the Russ and the Greeks, which I have already mentioned, also prove the great importance of the Russian trade, their chief purpose being to stipulate for the commercial privileges of the Russ; it is even possible that the later expeditions of the Russ against Greece were undertaken principally to secure those privileges[2].

Add to this that from the beginning of the tenth century the Russ often served in the Greek army and navy[3], and you will see that the Greeks had plenty of opportunities of becoming acquainted with that

[1] Comp. Rambaud, L'Empire Grec, pp. 386-387.

[2] Ibid., p. 374 f.

[3] Kunik in Mémoires de l'Acad. Imp. des sciences de St. Pétersbourg, vii⁰ série, tome xxiii. p. 36. Rambaud, L'Empire Grec, p. 387-390.

people. It is therefore no wonder that we exceedingly often find the '*Rhôs*' mentioned by Byzantine authors, and that we owe to the intercourse of the Russ with the Greeks some of the most decisive proofs of their Scandinavian nationality, which I shall mention in my next lecture.

Besides the Greeks there is another group of writers who give us much information with respect to the ancient Russ. I mean the Arabian, or rather the Mahomedan, authors; and the name by which they mention the Russ is *Rûs* (روس)[1].

The sketch of this tribe which the Oriental authors give us corresponds exactly with that presented to us by Greek writers. We find them represented as an extremely active, restless, and fool-hardy people, who, braving all dangers and difficulties, pressed forward far into the unknown regions of the East. Now they appear as peaceful merchants, now as bloodthirsty warriors who, like a flash of lightning, suddenly fall upon the unsuspecting inhabitants, plundering and murdering them, or carrying them away into captivity. Unlike the other warlike tribes who in those times were a terror to their neighbours, they never approached them by land, but always by sea, their only conveyance being their ships. From the land lying round the sources of the Volga they descended that river and traded with the Bulgarians; by the

---

[1] The notices upon the Russ and the Slavonians which are found in Mahomedan authors, are collected and translated into Russian by A. Harkavy in his book : Сказанія мусульманскихъ писателей о Славянахъ и Русскихъ. Собралъ, перевелъ и объяснялъ А. Я. Гаркави. Санктпетербургъ, 1870.

Dnieper they reached the Black Sea, which from about 900 to 1223 even bore the name of the Russian Sea, 'because, as Masudi the Arab (c. 940) says, none but the Russ navigate it.' But they did not even stop there. Through the Volga, which they sometimes reached from the Black Sea and the Sea of Azov by sailing up the Don and thence crossing to that river, they forced their way into the Caspian Sea. The first time they infested those regions was as early as c. 880. During the next hundred years the Russ undertook several expeditions thither, often in great swarms; thus we read in Masudi that in the year 913 they appeared in the Caspian Sea with a fleet of 500 ships, each containing 100 men.

It is worth noticing how early the expeditions of the Russ to these lands began, and how rapidly their name became known and feared in the East also. There is however nothing unreasonable in this, when we remember that even in 865 the Russ had ventured so far as to attack Constantinople. Yet nearly twenty years elapse from the date fixed by Nestor for the establishment of the Russian state, before the Oriental nations made acquaintance with that people.

On the other side it deserves notice that we do not find the Russ referred to by Oriental writers before that time. It is true, there were very few historical and geographical writers among the Arabs before that period; nevertheless there are at least five or six authors who mention the Slavs[1], but none of them

---

[1] The usual Arabian name of the Slavs is *Saklab* (صقلاب, صقلب), plural *Sakálibah* (صقالبة), a form which is evidently borrowed from the Greek Σκλάβοι.

say a single word of the Russ. The most ancient of the Mahomedan authors who mention them wrote about the year 900 [1].

Some of these authors have bequeathed to us most interesting sketches of manners and customs in ancient Russia. One of the earliest of these writers is Ibn Dustah (c. 912 A. D.) [2]. He tells us: 'The Russ dwell on a marshy island, surrounded by a lake, three days' journey (about 60 English miles) in circumference, and covered with swamps and forests; it is extremely unhealthy, and so marshy that the earth quivers when the foot is set to the ground. They have a prince who is called *Khakan-Rûs.* They attack the Slavs by ship, take them prisoner, and afterwards carry them to the Khazars and Bulgarians and sell them as slaves. They have no cornfields, but live on what they can plunder from the Slavs.

---

[1] The anti-Scandinavianists thought they had found a far earlier reference to the Russ. It was a passage in a Persian translation of an historical work by the Arabian Tabary, where, under the date of the year 643, a people is spoken of called *Rûs,* ' the enemies of all the world, especially of the Arabs,' as it is expressed. This passage has been quoted as a proof that the Russ had dwelt somewhere north of the Black Sea or the Caspian Sea long before the date given by Nestor. The passage in question, however, proves nothing; for it has been proved that this notice of the *Rûs* does not appear in the corresponding place in the Arabian original of Tabary himself. It was consequently interpolated by the Persian translator who wrote c. 963, and in whose time the Oriental nations had had ample opportunity to become acquainted with the Russ. See Dorn's Caspia, Mémoires de l'Acad. Impér. des sciences de St. Pétersbourg, vii° série, tome xxiii. p. 28 ff., and Kunik, ibid., p. 233 ff.

[2] Published by Chwolson under the title: Извѣстія о Хозарахъ, Буртасахъ, Болгарахъ, Мадьярахъ, Славянахъ и Руссахъ Ибнъ-Даста. Санктпетб., 1869. Compare Harkavy, l. c. p. 260 ff., and Catalogus codicum manuscr. orientalium qui in Museo Britannico asservantur, pars ii. pp. 604-607. London, 1871, fol.

When a son is born to any one of them, the father
throws a sword at him, saying, "I do not leave thee
any property; thine is only what thou gainest with thy
sword." They have neither real property nor towns
nor fields; their only occupation is trading in all sorts
of fur; they keep in their belts the money they
receive for it. The men wear gold bracelets. If
any of their tribes want assistance, all of them take
the field; they do not separate, but fight unanimously
against the enemy until they vanquish him. When
any one goes to law with another, they plead before
the king, and when the king has passed sentence, what
he orders is performed. But when neither of the
parties is satisfied with his decision, he orders them
to settle the matter themselves with their swords : he
whose sword is the sharper gains the cause. They
are courageous and brave. When they attack another
people, they do not cease till they have completely
destroyed them; they ravish the vanquished, and
make slaves of them. They are tall and look well,
and show great boldness in their attacks; however,
they do not exhibit their boldness on horseback, but
undertake all their expeditions and attacks in ships.
. . . They always wear their swords, because they have
but little confidence in each other, and because fraud
is very common among them; if any one succeed in
acquiring property, to ever so slight an amount, even
his brother or comrade immediately will envy him,
and watch for an opportunity to kill and plunder him.
When a man of quality dies, they make him a tomb
in the shape of a large house, put him in there, and
together with him they put into the same tomb his

clothes as well as the gold bracelets he has worn, and a quantity of victuals and vessels with drink and coins. Finally they put the favourite wife of the deceased alive into the barrow, fill up the entrance, and the woman dies in the enclosure.'

For the present I will only call your attention to the contrast, in Ibn Dustah's account, between the Russ themselves and the Slavs on whom they made war. Next we must observe that Ibn Dustah's sketch of the Russ in reality does not at all answer to their mode of living in his day; for then they dwelt in Kiev, and not upon an unhealthy remote island, and at that time their state was completely organized, politically speaking, and they were no mere plunderers as he has represented them.

It appears to me that we here have a statement from a second, perhaps even a third hand, the source of which dates from the time before the foundation of the Russian state, at which period the dwellings and mode of living of the Russ may have been such as he describes them. When the author says that their prince was called *Khakan-Rûs*, it seems to suggest that he may have derived his statement, directly or indirectly, from the Khazars, as *Khakan* is a Turkish or Tatar title which was really applied to their own princes by the Khazars themselves[1].

Another Arabian author who gives us a most remarkable, though in several points certainly exaggerated and uncritical, account of the Russ, is Ibn Fadhlan. In 921 and 922 he was sent to the Volga-

[1] Comp. A. Hatzuk in Труды перваго археолог. съѣзда въ Москвѣ. 1869, vol. i. p. 145 f.

Bulgarians as ambassador from the Kalif Muktadir,
and during his stay there he often had an opportunity
of seing the Russ when they came down the Volga to
trade with the Bulgarians. Of this journey he left
a description, of which fragments are preserved in the
Geographical Dictionary of Yakut, under the article
Rûs[1].

'I saw the Russ,' says Ibn Fadhlan, 'who had
arrived with their wares, and had encamped upon the
river Itil (Volga). Never saw I people of more perfect stature; they are tall like palm-trees, ruddy and
fair-haired. They clothe themselves neither in jackets
nor in kaftans, but the men wear a coarse cloak,
which they throw over the one side, so that one of
their hands is left free. Every man carries an axe,
a knife, and a sword. Without these weapons they
are never seen. Their swords are broad, streaked with
wavy lines, and of Frankish workmanship. . . . . The
women wear on the bosom a small capsule of iron,
copper, silver, or gold, according to the wealth and
standing of the husband. On the capsule is a ring,
and on that a knife, fastened equally on the bosom.
Round the neck they wear gold and silver chains.
When a man possesses ten thousand dirhems (silver
coins), he has a chain made for his wife; if he has
twenty thousand, she gets two neck-chains, and in
that way, as often as he becomes ten thousand dirhems richer, his wife receives another chain. Therefore a Russian woman often wears a great many
chains round her neck. Their greatest ornament

---

1 Frähn, Ibn-Foszlan's und anderer Araber Berichte über die Russen
älterer Zeit. St. Petersburg, 1823, 4to.

consists of green glass beads, such as may be found
in ships. They are very fond of them, and will pay a
dirhem a piece for them and string them as neck-
chains for their wives. They are the most uncleanly
men that God has created. . . . They come from their
country, anchor their ships in the Itil, which is a large
river, and build on its shores large booths of wood.
In such a booth ten or twenty of them live together,
and each of them has a settle. . . . As soon as their
ships have arrived at the anchoring-place, each of
them goes on shore, taking with him bread, meat,
onions, milk and spirituous drinks, and proceeds to an
erect high pole carved to resemble a human face, and
surrounded by small images, behind which other high
poles are erected. When he arrives at the high
wooden figure, he prostrates himself before it, saying :
Oh, my Lord, I have come from afar and bring with
me so many girls and so many sables. Having
enumerated in this way all the wares he has brought,
he continues : This present I have brought to thee.
Then he leaves before the wooden image what he has
brought, saying : I pray thee to grant me a purchaser
well provided with gold and silver coins, who will buy
all as I wish without bargaining. Having said this
he goes off. When his business goes wrong and
the time seems long to him, he comes back bringing
a second and even a third present. If he cannot yet
attain what he wishes, he brings a present for each
of the small images, and entreats their intercession,
saying : Are not these our Lord's wives, daughters
and sons ? If his business then prospers, and he
sells all his wares, he says : My Lord has fulfilled my

D

wish ; now it is my duty to make him a return.
Then he offers to the gods a sacrifice of many oxen
and sheep.'

Now follows a description of the funeral of a
Russian chieftain, but it is too long to be given here
in extenso. A chieftain of the Russ died during
their stay there. First his slaves were asked, which
of them would die with him? and one of the girls
declared herself willing to do so. On the day of the
funeral the corpse was taken on board the ship, and
placed there within a kind of tent. Beside him were
laid his weapon, and the bodies of several victims,
among others two horses. Finally, the girl too was
led thither and killed. Then the ship was set on
fire, and ere an hour elapsed, all, both ship and
corpses, had become the prey of the flames, and were
reduced to ashes.

However interesting these different accounts of the
Russ may be, as evidence of the manners and customs
of ancient Russia, they cast generally but little light
on the question of the nationality of the Russ. The
vague signification which the Oriental nations gradually attached to the name *Rûs*, is one of the
reasons for this. For it is evident that they very
soon began to apply this name not only to the Russ
properly speaking, but to all the people who belonged
to the Russian kingdom, were they Scandinavians,
Slavs, or Finns, that is, to all who came eastwards
from beyond the Bulgarians and Khazars. We find
a clear indication of this application of the word in
a notice which is to be met with in several Arabian
authors of the tenth century (the earliest being, it

appears, either Abu-Iskhak al-Istakhri or Abu-Zaid al-Balkhi, both c. 950. A.D.)[1]. They say as follows: 'The *Rûs* are divided into three tribes. The one is nearest the Bulgarians, and their king dwells in a town called *Kuyabah* (Kiev) which is larger than Bulgar. The second and more remote tribe is called *Selâviyah;* the third is called *Artaniah* (or *Barmaniah?*) and its king lives in *Arta* (?).' The first of the three tribes is evidently the Russ proper in Kiev; the second are Slavs, chiefly those of Novgorod; by the third is probably meant some Finnish tribe, but which of these is particularly referred to, is doubtful; whether the *Ersa*-Mordwins (?) or the *Permians*, in Anglo-Saxon *Beormas*, in Old Norse *Bjarmar*(?).

On account of the uncertainty which reigns in the terminology of Oriental authors, it cannot be doubted that many of the notices they give us of manners and customs in Russia, do not really refer to the Russ themselves, but now to one now to another of the tribes which were comprised under this name. Any theory whatever that has been proposed with regard to the nationality of the Russ has therefore been able to find specious support in Oriental authors. Under these circumstances it is necessary to use these writings with great caution, all the more as they certainly contain several exaggerations or misapprehensions. It is, however, incontestable that there are notices which can only apply to the Scandinavians,

---

[1] Frähn, Ibn-Foszlan, p. 141 ff. Harkavy, Сказаніа &c., pp. 193, 197 ff., 276, &c. Chwolson, in Труды перваго археолог. съѣзда въ Москвѣ. 1869, i. p. 133 f.

and therefore may be properly used to support Nestor's account of the origin of the Russ.

I will return to this point in the next lecture, when I will review the evidence produced from different sources to prove that the Russ really were Scandinavians.

LECTURE II.

IN the preceding lecture I sought to take a survey
of the ethnography of ancient Russia; I gave you
Nestor's relation of the foundation of the Russian
state, and I added a description of its founders, the
Russ, derived from Greek and Oriental sources.

I am now going to lay before you evidence from
other sources to corroborate Nestor's account of the
Scandinavian origin of the Russ. I freely confess that
most of this evidence is by no means new; but con-
sidering the opposition which has been raised against
this view, it cannot be too often repeated, and I
hope also to be able to present to you fresher and
more correct views as to some of the details of the
subject than have hitherto been entertained.

As I have mentioned before, the Greek form of the
name Russ is *Rhôs*, 'Ρῶς (or *Rusiai*, 'Ρούσιοι), and from
the close of the ninth century Byzantine literature
abounds in references to the Rhos. There is no doubt
that the Greeks were thoroughly acquainted with this
people, and it is evident that they well knew how to
distinguish them from other neighbouring nations and
particularly from the Slavs. But if we ask for the
real nationality of the people to whom the Greeks
applied the name *Rhôs*, Byzantine literature itself

gives us no direct and positive answer. A designation
of them which sometimes occurs, is *Scyths* (Σκυθαί)
or *Tauroscyths* (Ταυροσκυθαί); but that is a learned
name, not a popular one, referring only to their
dwelling in the territory of the ancient Scyths, north
of the Black Sea, without reference to their nationality.
A few of the Byzantine authors give us a little more
definite suggestion on this subject, inasmuch as, in
mentioning the expedition of 941, they design the
Rhos as 'being of the race of the *Franks,*' i.e. of
Teutonic race, for in this general signification the
name Franks is sometimes used by the Byzantines [1].

But fortunately there are other ways of supplying
this want. I shall begin by reviewing a series of
passages from mediæval authors of Western Europe,
which give us precise information upon the ethnographical meaning of the Greek word *Rhôs.* The unanimous testimony of these documents is that by this
name the Greeks denoted the same people which elsewhere in Europe was so well known under the common
name of *Northmen.*

The first time we find the *Rhos* mentioned is in the

---

[1] Leontios (continuator Theophanis) in describing the expedition of
941 mentions οἱ Ῥῶς οἱ καὶ Δρομῖται λεγόμενοι. οἱ ἐκ γένους τῶν Φράγγων
καθίστανται. Exactly the same expressions are used by Georgios Hamar-
tolos in an unedited manuscript in the Vatican library (Gedeonov, O
варяжскомъ вопросѣ, i. p. 74), and by the so-called Simeon Logothetes
who certainly has transcribed Leontios. Comp. Kunik, Berufung der
schwed. Rodsen, ii. p. 394 ff., 409 ff. On the Byzantine use of the word
Franks comp. Kunik, l. c. p. 388, and Mémoires de l'Acad. Imp. de
St. Pétersbourg, vii série, tome xxiii. p. 29. The name *Dromitai* is explained by Kunik, Beruf. ii. p. 405, O записке готскаго топарха, in the
Записки Акад. Наукъ, xxiv. p. 114 ff., and in Mémoires de l'Acad. Imp.,
vii série, xxiii. p. 400.

so-called *Annales Bertiniani* for the year 839 [1]. The portion of these annals in which this notice is found, and which includes the years from 835 to 861, is due to the bishop of Troyes, Prudentius, a learned and conscientious man, whose work ranks among the best and most trustworthy of that time. He tells us that in the year 839 there came to the emperor Louis the Pious Greek ambassadors, sent by the Byzantine emperor Theophilos, who brought with them a letter, together with costly presents. The emperor received them most honourably at Ingelheim on the 18th May. Together with them, continues Prudentius, he sent some persons 'who said that they, —that is to say their nation,—were called *Rhos*, and whom their own king, Chacanus by name, had sent to him for friendship's sake, as they asserted;' now he begged the emperor in the said letter, that they might travel under his protection through the whole of his empire, as he would not allow them to return by the same way they had come, because they were obliged to pass through rough and barbarous tribes of the utmost ferocity. But inquiring more exactly the reason of their coming, *he learned that they were of Swedish nationality*, and supposing that they had come rather as spies than in search of friendship, he resolved to detain them near him, until he could discover whether their intention were honest or not.

---

[1] The first who called attention to this passage was Th. S. Bayer in his Origines Russicae (Commentationes Academiae Scient. Petropolitanae, viii 1736, p. 388). Since then it has been discussed innumerable times. See especially Kunik, Die Berufung der schwed. Rodsen, ii. p. 195 ff.

Hereupon he sent information to the Greek emperor
through his ambassadors[1].

The meaning of this passage seems to me to be
quite clear. The people whose king sent ambassadors
to the Greek emperor, and with whose existence the
Greeks perhaps for the first time became acquainted,
was called Rhos at Constantinople; whether they
really used this name in their own language, or only
were called so by others, is a question to which I
shall afterwards return; here it is of no consequence.
Under the same name, Rhos, the emperor Theophilos
in his turn introduced them to Louis the Pious in the
letter with which he had furnished his ambassadors,
and which was of course written in Greek. That
Prudentius refers to this letter is evident from his
writing *Rhos*, that plainly gives us the Greek form

---

[1] ' Venerunt legati Graecorum a Theophilo imperatore directi . . . .
ferentes cum donis imperatore dignis epistolam; quos imperator quinto
decimo Kal. Junii in Ingulenheim honorifice suscepit. . . . Misit
etiam cum eis quosdam *qui se, id est gentem suam, Rhos vocari dicebant,*
quos rex illorum, Chacanus vocabulo, ad se amicitiae, sicut asserebant,
causa direxerat, petens per memoratam epistolam, quatenus benignitate
imperatoris redeundi facultatem atque auxilium per imperium suum
totum habere possent, quoniam itinera per quae ad illum Constantinopolim venerant, inter barbaras et nimiae feritatis gentes immanissimas
habuerant, quibus eos, ne forte periculum inciderent, redire noluit.
Quorum adventus causam imperator diligentius investigans, *comperit eos*
gentis esse Sueonum, exploratores potius regni illius nostrique quam
amicitiae petitores ratus, penes se eo usque retinendos judicavit quod
veraciter invenire posset, utrum fideliter eo necne pervenerint; idque
Theophilo per memoratos legatos suos atque epistolam intimare non
distulit, et quod eos illius amore libenter susceperit; ac si fideles inveni-
rentur, et facultas absque illorum periculo in patriam remeandi daretur,
cum auxilio remittendos; sin alias, una cum missis nostris ad ejus prae-
sentiam dirigendos, ut, quid de talibus fieri deberet, ipse decernendo
efficeret.' Pertz, Monumenta Germ. Hist., Script., i. p. 434.

'Ρῶς [1]. But this name being at that time yet unknown in the whole of the West, it was necessary to make more exact inquiries of the ambassadors, and the result was that those persons who in the letter of the Greek emperor were designated as Rhos, and consequently belonged to a branch of those Northmen whom the Franks at that time knew but too well, and had every reason to suspect. Herein lies, then, the very natural explanation of the emperor's precautions against them. The inference to be drawn from this passage consequently is, that *Rhos*, 'Ρῶς, was the Greek name of the Swedes.

It is not said where the home of those Rhos was situated. It was perhaps somewhere in Sweden itself; but it might be, too, that we have to do here with some emigrated tribe, already settled beyond the Baltic or the Gulf of Bothnia. At any rate, the ambassadors had evidently gone to Greece through what is now Russia, probably by the Dnieper, and it was by this road, really infested by a number of barbarous tribes, that the emperor would not allow them to return.

One thing is remarkable, namely, that the king of the Rhos is said to be called *Chacanus.* It has been very much disputed whether this is his name or his title. I have no doubt, however, that, at least in the original Greek letter, it was meant to be the title *khagan* or *khakan*, which I have mentioned several times in the first lecture. But if we will ask how the

---

[1] Compare also the expression ' quos rex ad se direxerat,' where the word *se* shows that this notice is not due to Prudentius himself, but is a quotation of the words of the Greek emperor.

Greek court came to give him this foreign title, there is certainly a wide scope for guessing. The most probable explanation is, it seems to me, that the Greeks confounded the Rhos with the Khazars, Avars, and other northern barbaric tribes[1], and therefore applied to the king of the Rhos the same title which the king of the Khazars bore[2]. This is so much the less to be wondered at, as these Swedes can only have reached the Black Sea through the land of the Khazars, and may even have been conducted to Constantinople and introduced at the Byzantine court by Khazars. In any case, no inference can be drawn from this appellation with respect to the nationality of the Rhos.

I cannot omit briefly to refer to the attempts of the anti-Scandinavianists to weaken this proof of the signification of the name Rhos. They cannot, of course, deny that the persons spoken of by Prudentius

---

[1] Compare a passage as this: εἴτε Χάζηροι εἴτε Τοῦρκοι εἴτε καὶ Ῥῶς ἢ ἕτερόν τι ἔθνος τῶν βορείων καὶ Σκυθικῶν, Constantine Porphyrogen., de administrando Imperio, ed. Bonn. p. 82.

[2] The same usage is suggested by a letter from Louis II, written in 871 to the Greek emperor Basilios, in which he rejects the protest of the latter against the Frankish kings calling themselves emperors, and protests, in his turn, against the claim the Greek emperors laid to the monopoly of the title βασιλεύς (' βασυλέως vocabulum '); he reproaches them because they refused to call foreign kings so, and applied for instance the title *chaganus* to the kings of the Avars, the Gazans or the Northmen (' praelatum Avarum, Gazanorum aut Nortmannorum ' — the last name answering evidently to the Greek τῶν Ῥῶς). See Pertz, Monumenta Germ. Hist., vol. iii. p. 523. Comp. the above mentioned notice in Ibn Dustah upon *Khakan-Rûs* (p. 31), which may also have passed through a Greek authority. It is only much later, after the complete destruction of the Khazarian empire, that we find some solitary instances of the title *kagan* being applied in Slavonic documents to the Russian grand-dukes Vladimir (+ 1015) and Yaroslav (+ 1054).

are Swedes, and their object therefore must be to show that the passage in question does not prove the identity of the names Rhos and Swedes; but, on the contrary, suggests a difference between them. The attempted explanations which have been given to this effect are extremely far-fetched. On one hand, it has been asserted that these persons may have been Swedes who, coming accidentally to Constantinople, had taken it into their heads to give themselves out to be ambassadors from the king of the Rhos, and that the Frankish emperor may have been the first to discover how matters stood. But this supposition is not borne out by any statement in the document itself. It is, on the contrary, highly improbable. Why should they take it into their heads to give themselves out to be ambassadors? It has been replied that, of course, their intention was fraudulently to obtain for themselves such presents as it was customary to offer to ambassadors. But even if that be the case, why did they not represent themselves to be ambassadors from their own nation instead of another? They could as well, or even better, have obtained the supposed advantages of their deception without such double masquerading, by which, indeed, they really gained nothing, but only made the part they tried to play doubly difficult and the danger of discovery doubly great. This supposition is in the highest degree far-fetched and improbable. According to another theory, which was first propounded in the last century, and has been lately revived by Gedeonov, these persons are supposed to be Swedes who were accidentally serving at the court of 'the

Russian Khagan,' and were sent by him as ambassadors to Constantinople ; they had, therefore, a
perfect right to represent themselves, in Constantinople, to be Rhos, though they themselves really
belonged to another nationality. But this explanation
is as untenable as it is far-fetched. In the first place,
it is quite opposed to Prudentius' plain words, as the
expressions ' qui se id est *gentem suam Rhos* vocari dicebant,' and ' eos *gentis* esse *Sueonum,*' are quite parallel,
and it is also said that it is their own king (rex illorum)
who sent them. In the next place, this interpretation
is entirely opposed to the customs and ideas of that
period, and leaves unexplained the question which in
that case must first and foremost be cleared up, viz.
how, in the ninth century, in an epoch when it was
an unheard-of thing that Scandinavians should take
service under a foreign non-Scandinavian prince, a
' Russian' (i. e. Slavonic) ' Khagan' in Kiev should
employ Swedes as his ambassadors. Such a circumstance would necessarily suggest a relationship between
the Russ and the Swedes ; and consequently, even if
this hypothesis were not in itself untenable, the conclusion to be drawn from it, at all events, would be quite
other than that which its propounders would desire.

I am convinced that every impartial reader will see at
once how strained and forced these explanations are,
and acknowledge that the only simple and natural interpretation of the passage in Prudentius is, that Rhos
was the Greek designation for the Scandinavians or
Northmen, who in this case happened to be Swedes.
This passage is the most ancient in which the name
Russ is mentioned, and it is the only occasion on

which we meet with it before Rurik's time. The
conclusion we draw from it is most evidently corroborated by documents of a rather more recent date.
There are several Latin writers who in mentioning
some of the expeditions of the Russ against Constantinople, expressly identify them with the people who,
in the Roman-Teutonic world, were called *Normanni.*

Of the expedition which took place in 865, Venetian
chronicles have preserved some short notices[1]. It is
true, the oldest of these chronicles is more than a
century younger than the event itself; it is written by
Johannes Diaconus, who lived at the close of the tenth
and the beginning of the eleventh century. But just
as the notice given by him has again been transcribed
by later chroniclers, so there can be no doubt that it
is founded on an authentic contemporary account.
It must be remembered, as Mr. Kunik observes, that
the Venetians, from an early date, carried on an extensive trade in the Mediterranean, and that above all
they held lively commercial and diplomatic intercourse with the capital of the Byzantine empire which
exercised even at those times, at least in name, a
sort of supremacy over the proud republic. Under
these circumstances, the almost incredible event
which took place in that year, the attack of Russian
pirates on Constantinople itself, must very early
have become known at Venice, from citizens who had
been eye-witnesses of it, and from some such account
the notice of the chronicler Johannes Diaconus must
have been derived. He says, without stating the year,
but in connection with events which took place about

---

[1] Kunik, Mémoires de l'Acad. Imp., vii. série, tome xxiii. pp. 230–232.

865, that 'at that time Northmen ventured to attack
the city of Constantinople with 360 vessels; but not
being able to injure the impregnable city itself, they
fought gallantly in the suburbs and killed as many
people as possible, after which they returned home in
triumph[1].' Notwithstanding some difference between
the details in this account and that of Nestor and the
Byzantine authors, it is obvious that the Northmen of
Johannes Diaconus and the Rhos of the Greeks are
identical; no other people of that period will answer
to the description.

If, nevertheless, any one should call this conclusion
in question, every doubt must vanish, if we compare a
passage or two of another Italian author, the Lombard
Liudprand, who from 963 was bishop of Cremona. He
had been twice at Constantinople, first between the
years 948 and 950 as ambassador from king Berenga-
rius II, and afterwards for four months in 968 as ambassador from the emperor Otto I. Consequently he
had had a good opportunity of making himself familiar with the affairs of the Byzantine empire, and the
accounts he has left us of his travels contain many
important statements as to this subject.

---

[1] 'Eo tempore Normannorum gentes cum trecentis sexaginta navibus
Constantinopolitanam urbem adire ausi sunt. Verum quia nulla racione
inexpugnabilem ledere valebant urbem, suburbanum fortiter patrantes
bellum quam plurimos ibi occidere non pepercerunt, et sic predicta gens
cum triumpho ad propriam regressa est.' (Pertz, Monumenta Germ.
Hist., Script., vii. p. 18.) With almost the same words, evidently based
upon the account of Johannes Diaconus, the event is related by the
Doge Andrew Dandulo (+1354) in his Chronicum Venetum, lib. viii.
c. 4. pars 41 (Muratori, Rerum Ital. Scriptores, xii. p. 181. Mediolani,
1728, fol.): 'Per haec tempora Normannorum gentes CCCLX navibus
aggressi sunt Constantinopolim, et suburbana impugnant multosque
occidunt et cum gloria redeunt.'

In one place he enumerates the nations that lived
north of the Greek empire, and among them he also
mentions 'the Russ (*Rusii*) whom we with another name
call Northmen [1].' In another place he gives us a description of the unfortunate expedition of Igor in 941,
quoting as his authority his own step-father who at
that time had been present at Constantinople as the
ambassador of the Italian king Hugo, and who with
his own eyes had seen Russian prisoners decapitated by
command of the Greek emperor Romanos. Here he
uses almost the same expressions about the Russ,
saying: 'There is a people living in the north, whom
from some personal quality the Greeks call *Rusii*[2],
while from the situation of their native place we call
them Northmen. King of this people was Inger, who
came to Constantinople with more than a thousand
vessels, &c.[3]'

[1] 'Habet quippe (Constantinopolis) ab aquilone Hungarios, Pizenacos,
Chazaros, Rusios quos alio nos nomine Nordmannos appellamus, atque
Bulgaros nimium sibi vicinos.' Pertz, Monumenta Germ. Hist., Scrip-
tores, vol. iii. p. 277.

[2] This remark is founded on a wrong etymology, the name of the
Russ being confounded with the Greek adjective ῥούσιοs, 'red, red-haired.'

[3] 'Quoniam meus vitricus, vir gravitate ornatus, plenus sapientia,
regis Hugonis fuerat nuntius, pigrum michi non hic sit inserere quid eum
de imperatoris sapientia et humanitate, et qualiter Rusios viceri*, audivi
sepius dicere. Gens quaedam est sub aquilonis parte constituta quam a
qualitate corporis Greci vocant *Rusios*, nos vero a positione loci nomina-
mus *Nordmannos*. Lingua quippe Teutonum *Nord* aquilo, *man* autem
dicitur homo, unde et Nordmannos aquilonares homines dicere pos-
sumus. Hujus denique gentis rex vocabulo *Inger* erat, qui collectis
mille et eo amplius navibus Constantinopolim venit. . . . Inger ingenti
cum confusione postmodum ad propria est reversus. Greci vero victoria
potiti, vivos secum multos ducentes, Constantinopolim regressi sunt laeti,
quos omnes Romanús in praesentia Hugonis nuntii, vitrici scilicet mei,
decollari praecepit.' Pertz, Monum. iii. p. 331.

These words are perfectly clear, and leave no doubt as to the signification still borne by the name Russ among the Greeks in Liudprand's time. The efforts made to elude this proof are of such a nature that it is unnecessary for me to refute them in detail. On the one hand, it is affirmed that the name *Northmen* might very well have been applied to the Slavs, as they also dwelt in the north. But this is absolutely false, for *Northmen*, *Normanni* was, in the middle ages, the specific denomination of the Scandinavians[1]; just as in our days, for instance, 'the North Sea' designates a particular sea, not any sea whatever which may happen to lie in the north. On the other hand, the supposition is brought forward that the Russ who were executed in the presence of Liudprand's step-father were perhaps merely Scandinavian auxiliaries serving in the Russian army, and that he may hence have concluded that all Russ were Northmen. But the information Liudprand received from his step-father is merely an intelligence of the victory of the Greeks over the Russ, and the revenge they took upon them ; as far as their nationality is concerned, he had ample opportunity of forming his own opinion, as he in several passages speaks of having seen them during his stay in Greece. The whole of this argument is based on such frivolous scepticism that there is nothing in the world that might not be called in question with such unscientific reasoning.

Thus, from the passages already quoted we see that the name *Rhos* ('Ρῶς) or *Rusioi* ('Ρούσιοι) was employed

---

[1] Comp. Joh. Steenstrup, Normannerne. I. Indledning i Normanner-tiden, p. 50 ff. Kjöbenhavn, 1876.

by the Greeks in the ninth and tenth centuries to designate the same nation which, in Western Europe, was
generally called *Normanni,* i.e. Northmen or Scandinavians; the latter name being as little known among
the Greeks as the former was in Western Europe.
But the name *Rhos, Rusioi,* the Slavonic *Rus',* belongs,
geographically speaking, κατ' ἐξοχὴν to the ruling tribe
in Kiev, and, consequently, this same tribe can only
have been an eastern ramification of the Northmen,—
the sole representatives of that nationality with whom
the Greeks had an opportunity of becoming acquainted.

Before proceeding to speak of that highly important
passage in a Greek author which gives us a most
decisive proof of this fact, I will first cast a glance at
the mention made of the Russ or *Rûs* by Oriental
authors. What we can adduce from them is, however,
of inferior value, in comparison with what we owe to
the Greeks.

I have before mentioned that the Oriental authors
use the name *Rûs* in so vague and uncertain a
manner that we can scarcely draw any decisive
inference from them as to the nationality of the
people to which this name properly belonged. On
this point it is evident the Orientals themselves had
but very indistinct ideas.

It is nevertheless incontestable that many passages
occur in which the Rûs are not only distinguished
from the Slavs, but are also characterised in a
manner that can apply to the Scandinavians alone.
I will only remind you of what is told us by Ibn
Dustah of the mode of living and manners of the
Russ: how they dwelt in a marshy island, how they

E

piratically attacked the Slavs, and how they only
engaged in trade and war; how they made all their
expeditions by ship instead of on horseback; also
how he describes their internal strife and contentions,
while, at the same time, they displayed implicit
obedience and concord when in the presence of their
enemies; how he draws their duels, their courage,
their cruelty to the conquered, their tall stature, their
beauty, &c.[1] The same may be said of several passages in Ibn Fadhlan's description of the Russ; for he
depicts them as 'tall like palm-trees, ruddy and fair-
haired, armed with axes, swords and knives of
Frankish workmanship;' and though some of the other
characteristic traits of the mode of living of the Russ
adduced by him are certainly somewhat exaggerated
and embellished, yet unquestionably under several of
them we catch glimpses of manners and customs especially peculiar to the Scandinavians; as, for instance,
where he describes, evidently somewhat fantastically,
how the body of a chieftain was placed upon a ship
and burnt. From all this it is clear that, however
indefinite the application of this name Russ by the
Mahomedan authors may be, there can be no doubt
that it is applied chiefly to the Scandinavians. There
can, therefore, be no doubt that the name Russ, when
it first reached the Mahomedans, bore the same signification as the corresponding name in Slavonic and
Greek, viz. a designation of the Northmen, especially
of those who had settled in Russia.

There is only one passage in an Arabian author in

[1] Comp. especially Steenstrup, Indledning i Normannertiden, pp.
263 ff., 351 ff., 289 f., 325 ff., 367 ff., 143, 361.

which the Russ are clearly identified with the Northmen. It is by Ahmed al-Ya'kûbi al-Kâtib, an author
who wrote shortly after the year 890[1]. He says that
in 844 'heathens (*Majûs*) who are called Rûs, attacked
Seville and plundered and ravaged, and burned and
murdered.' Now we learn elsewhere that the coasts
of Spain were really visited in that year by a host of
Northmen, who had previously ravaged different parts
of France, and it must be to them the author refers as
the people who are called Rûs. The question is, however, how came he to give this name to these Northmen? For, of course, they did not call themselves so.
Is this passage derived from some Greek authority?
or, rather, has not the author—or perhaps some later
transcriber—transferred the name Russ which, from
about A.D. 880, was well known in the East, to the
Northmen whose conduct in Spain was exactly similar
to that of the Russ on the coast of the Caspian and
the Black Sea? The Arabian Masudi (c. 920—950)
does so: after referring to this very attack of the
'heathens' on Spain he adds, as his own private
opinion: 'I believe that these people were Rûs: for
none but they sail on this sea (the Black sea) which
communicates with the ocean (*Ukianus*).' On account
of this doubt, therefore, neither the passage from
Ahmed al-Kâtib nor that from Masudi can be adduced as positive proof that the Russ, the Rûs of the
Arabians, were Northmen. Both these passages, however, show clearly that the Arabians themselves must

---

[1] See Frähn in Bulletin scientifique publ. p. l'Acad. Imp. de St.
Pétersbourg. Tome iv. No. 9, 10, 1838. Kunik, Berufung der Schwed.
Rodsen, vol. ii. p. 285 ff. Harkavy, Сказанія, &c., p. 59 ff.

have had an impression that the Northmen who devastated the west were the same people as those they called Rûs.

But I return to the Greeks, in order to mention one of the most remarkable and instructive passages upon the Russ which can be found in any contemporary author. It is the ninth chapter of the work of the emperor Constantine Porphyrogenitus on the administration of the Greek empire (de administrando Imperio), written about 950. This chapter is entitled 'Of the Rhos who come from Russia to Constantinople with their boats [1];' and what makes it so precious to us is the fact that it is the only document we have which gives us a direct specimen of the language of the ancient Russ.

The boats (μονύξυλα), he tells us, that go to Constantinople, from 'exterior Russia' (ἀπὸ τῆς ἔξω 'Ρωσίας, i. e. the land beyond Kiev), come from Novgorod (ἀπὸ τοῦ Νεμογαρδάς), from Smolensk (Μιλινίσκα), Lubetch (Τελιούτζα), Tchernigov (Τζερνιγώγα), and Vyshegrad (Βουσεγραδέ), and go down the Dnieper, until they meet near Kiev (Κιοάβα), which is also called *Sambatas* (Σαμβατάς). Here their number is considerably augmented by new boats, for which the materials have been floated down the lakes and rivers from the more woody territories of different Slavonic tribes which are tributary to the Rhos. When these boats have been fitted out, they start from Kiev in the month of June, after which all the boats assemble near the fortress Vytitchev (Βιτετζέβη) in order to pass in com-

---

[1] Περὶ τῶν ἀπὸ τῆς 'Ρωσίας ἐρχομένων 'Ρῶς μετὰ τῶν μονοξύλων ἐν Κωνσταντινουπόλει.

pany that long series of rapids (in modern Russian
porogi, literally, thresholds, dams), which the Dnieper
forms for a distance of about fifty English miles from a
little below the modern town of Yekaterinoslav[1]. It
was not nature only that made the passage of these
rapids dangerous, but they were also infested by
neighbouring tribes of depredatory nomads (especially
the Petchenegs), always ready for attack. The passage
therefore needed the utmost circumspection, and it
was not advisable to venture upon it save with a
numerous caravan. Of this passage Constantine gives
us a short description, enumerating seven of the
rapids and giving their names in two languages,
Slavonic (Σκλαβινιστί) and Russ ('Ρωσιστί). The explanation of these names has occupied philologers
and historians for more than a century[2]. The Slavonic names are really pure Slavonic, and some of
them completely agree with the modern Russian

[1] Comp. Description d'Ukranie qui sont plusieurs Prouinces du
Royaume de Pologne, &c., par le Sieur de Beauplan, pp. 19-21.
Rouen, 1660, 4to. Lehrberg, Untersuchungen zur Erläuterung der älteren
Geschichte Russlands, p. 319 ff. St. Petersburg, 1816, 4to. J. Ch.
Stuckenberg, Hydrographie des Russischen Reiches, iii. p. 252 ff. St.
Petersburg, 1847.

[2] Th. S. Bayer in Commentarii Academiae Scient. Imper. Petropolitanae, tom. ix. ad annum 1737 (1744), p. 392 ff. Strube, Disser-
tation sur les anciens Russes, 1785. J. Thunmann's Untersuchungen
über die Geschichte der östlichen europäischen Völker, vol. i. p. 386 ff.
Leipzig, 1774. Lehrberg, l. c., p. 350 ff. K. Zeuss, Die Deutschen
und die Nachbarstämme, p. 556 ff. München, 1837. Kunik, Die
Berufung der schwedischen Rodsen, vol. ii. pp. 425-438. P. A. Munch,
Samlede Afhandlinger udgivne af. G. Storm, vol. ii. p. 189 f. Christiania, 1874 (1849). C. Rafn, Antiquités de l'Orient, pp. vii-viii. Copenhague, 1856. Kunik in Mémoires de l'Acad. Imp. des Sciences de St.
Pétersbourg, vii° série, tome xxiii. pp. 414, 415. 1875.

names of the rapids, though the form in which Constantine has transmitted them to us is sometimes influenced by the Bulgarian or Old Slavonic idiom which must have been the most current among the different Slavonic idioms at the Byzantine court. But the other set of names, those which Constantine gives us as the Russ, are quite different from them, and form a group which is highly interesting to us and important for our purpose. For every one who has the least notion of languages and is not blinded by prejudice must own that they are pure Scandinavian, and cannot be explained through any other language.

I shall try to give an analysis of these names.

First, says the author, the travellers come to the rapid called *Essupi*, which in Russ and Slavonic signifies ' do not sleep' (πρῶτον μὲν ἔρχονται εἰς τὸν πρῶτον φραγμὸν τὸν ἐπονομαζόμενον Ἐσσουπῆ, ὃ ἑρμηνεύεται Ῥωσιστὶ καὶ Σκλαβινιστὶ μὴ κοιμᾶσθαι). Such a warning as is contained in these words would really be no unreasonable name for the first rapid with which the long series of dangers begins. One thing appears strange, when we compare this name with the following names : the author seems to suggest that the Russ and the Slavonic name were the same. But when we consider that all the other rapids have double names of a quite different nature, there can be no doubt that there must be an error in this passage, and that one of the names has been omitted. It has long been agreed that that given by Constantine is the Slavonic name. The pure Slavonic translation of the phrase ' do not sleep' is *ne s'pi* (не съпи);

and this form we really can obtain by a very slight change, if we suppose, as has been suggested long ago, *Essupi* to be miswritten for *Nessupi*. That an *n* has been dropped at the beginning of the word is all the more likely and excusable, as the preceding word of the text ends in *n*. What the Russ name was, we do not know; but as from all the following names we are entitled to suppose that it was of Scandinavian origin, it must, if it had the same form and signification as the Slavonic, have been something like *sof eigi* or *sofattu*, the Old Norse form of this phrase.

The second rapid is called in Russ *Ulvorsi*, in Slavonic *Ostrovuniprakh*, which is explained as 'the islet of the rapid' (κατέρχονται εἰς τὸν ἕτερον φραγμὸν τὸν ἐπιλεγόμενον Ῥωσιστὶ μὲν Οὐλβορσί, Σκλαβινιστὶ δὲ Ὀστροβουνίπραχ, ὅπερ ἑρμηνεύεται τὸ νησίον τοῦ φραγμοῦ). This name is quite clear. The Slavonic form is the Old Slavonic *ostrov'nyi prag'* (островьныи прагъ), *ostrov'nyi* being an adjective derived from *ostrov'*, an isle, and *prag'*, modern Russian *poróg'*, a rapid. Constantine's translation 'the islet of the rapid' is not quite correct; the words ought to be reversed: 'the Islet-fall.' The Russ name perfectly agrees with this interpretation. It is evidently the Scandinavian *Holm-fors*, a compound of the common Scandinavian word *holm*, Old Norse *hólmr*[1], a holm, an islet; and *fors* the Scandi-

---

[1] The Grecian form Οὐλ- may be compared with the lateral form *hulm*, which occurs in several old Swedish documents and still exists in some Swedish dialects. The nasal *m* may have been pronounced rather indistinctly before *f*; thus in several Runic inscriptions from Sweden the name *Holm-fastr* is written HULFASTR, for instance, in Dybeck

navian word for a waterfall, a rapid, 'a force.' Between
the first rapid, and that which Constantine gives us as
the third, there are in reality two rapids; the first
of them of which the modern name is *Surski*, is not
very important; but the second, now called *Lokhanski*,
is one of the most dangerous of them all. As these two
rapids succeed each other at a slight distance, it is
possible that both of them were comprised under the
ancient name '*Holm-force*.' As to the origin of this
name, it may have been derived either from three
rocky isles, situated just above the *Lokhanski*[1], or
rather from an isle, about one English mile long, and
covered with oaks and other trees, which is characteristic of the *Surski*[2].

With reference to the third rapid Constantine says
that it is called '*Gelandri*, which means in Slavonic
the resonance of the rapid' (τὸν τρίτον φραγμὸν τὸν
λεγόμενον Γελανδρί, ὃ ἑρμηνεύεται Σκλαβινιστὶ ἦχος φραγμοῦ). This passage has evidently been a little cor-
rupted; for not merely does it give us only one name,
but this one name must also have been assigned to the
wrong language. For *Gelandri* can be only the Old
Norse participle *gellandi* (or *gjallandi*), 'the echoing, the
resounding'[3]. The author consequently here makes a

Sverikes Runurkunder, 1860 ff., Upland, No. 18, 114, 140, etc. (ibid., No.
146, HULMNFASTR; ibid., Stockholmslän, No. 173, HULMFASTR).

[1] This is the opinion of Lehrberg, l. c., pp. 325, 356.

[2] 'Neben einer mit Eichen und anderen Bäumen bewaldeten Insel.'
Stuckenberg, l. c., p. 254. Comp. Lehrberg, l. c., p. 324.

[3] This name brings to mind similar names in the Scandinavian countries, as *Rjúkandi*, 'the reeking, smoking,' a waterfall in Norway;
Skjálfanda-fljót, 'the trembling river' in Iceland; *Rennandi*, 'the run-
ning,' a mythic river, in the Edda (Grímnismál 27) &c.

slight error in his translation, similar to the one he made in the preceding name, in so much that he renders *Gelandri* 'the resonance of the rapid' instead of 'the resounding rapid.' While in the account of the first rapid the Russ name is wanting, it is here the Slavonic name which has been omitted by the transcriber[1]. What it was, we cannot of course state with certainty, but in all probability it must have been something like the modern Russian name of this very rapid *Zvonets*, (*Zvonski, Zvonetski,*) which has just the same meaning as the one name given us, viz. 'the resounding.' At this place the water is said really to rush with such a noise and roaring, that it can be heard very far off[2].

After this we arrive at the fourth rapid, 'the large,' which is called in Russ *Aïfar*, in Slavonic *Neasit*, as Constantine says, because the pelicans have their nests on the stones of the rapid (τὸν τέταρτον φραγμόν,

---

[1] According to the conjecture of Kunik (l. c., ii. p. 430) the original wording of the text may have been: τὸν λεγόμενον ['Ρωσιστὶ μὲν] Γελανδρί, Σκλαβινιστὶ [δὲ . . .], ὃ ἑρμηνεύεται, &c.

[2] 'Hundert Faden unterhalb dieses Falles engt sich das Strombett bis auf 300 Faden ein, und die rauschenden, an die Felsen anprallenden Wogen verursachen ein solches Gebrause, dass es weit in die Ferne hallt. Vermuthlich rührt daher der Name des Swonetz d. h. des klingenden.' Stuckenberg, l. c., p. 254. Compare Lehrberg, l. c., p. 327, and W. Szujew, Beschreibung seiner Reise von St. Petersburg nach Cherson, i. p. 181 (Dresden and Leipzig, 1789), who writes: 'Wir trafen den Szwonezkischen Wasserfall, der sich uns schon von weiten durch sein Rauschen ankündigte. . . . . Um uns die langweilige Zeit zu verkürzen, verschafte der Szwonezkische Wasserfall mit dem unaufhörlichen weit umher erschallenden Brausen seiner durch die Klippen sich durcharbeitenden Wogen unserm Gehör Unterhaltung, und liess uns eine grosse Mannichfaltigkeit von Tönen vernehmen, die durch die bald mehr bald weniger gepresste Wasserströmung hervorgebracht wurden.'

τὸν μέγαν, τὸν ἐπιλεγόμενον Ῥωσιστὶ μὲν Ἀειφάρ, Σκλαβινιστὶ δὲ Νεασήτ, διότι φωλεύουσιν οἱ πελεκᾶνοι εἰς τὰ
λιθάρια τοῦ φραγμοῦ). As, in my opinion, the names of
this rapid have been hitherto completely misunder-
stood, I must dwell a little longer upon it. The rapid
itself is evidently that which is now called *Nenasytets*, a rapid which, according to all descriptions, is
the largest and most dangerous of them all[1].

As to the Slavonic designation *Neasit*, it is clear
enough, as it apparently represents the Old Slavonic
neyesyt' (неіасыть), in the Slavonic church language of
Russia *neyasyt'* (неіасыть), which does in fact signify a
pelican, and in this almost all previous interpreters
have acquiesced; in consequence of Constantine's
words they have therefore explained the name as
'the Pelican-fall.' But, strange to say, none of them,
so far as I know, have been aware of a difficulty
which, after all, seems to me to render this interpretation extremely doubtful. That is, that the name of
the rapid itself is said to be ' *Neasit* ' which, according
to this interpretation, must signify 'the Pelican,' not
'the Pelican-fall.' If the origin of the name were
really that which Constantine gives us, we should
necessarily expect in Slavonic some name derived
from ' *neasit*,' in a similar manner as the name of

---

[1] In the work of Stuckenberg (p. 254) it is shortly described thus:
'Durch eine eigene Verknüpfung von Widerständen und von Hinder-
nissen, welche sich hier, durch [zwei] Inseln, durch die Richtungen und
Biegungen des Fahrwassers und durch andere Oertlichkeiten bedingt,
dem Strome entgegenstellen, entsteht der Nenassitez, den die Schiffer mit
Recht einen Backofen oder die Hölle nennen.' For more details see
Szujew, Beschreibung seiner Reise, i. p. 183 f. and Lehrberg, l. c.,
p. 327 ff.

the second rapid is a derivative from *ostrov'*, and just as in English it would be necessary to use a compound name, as ' the Pelican-*fall.*' But every one will surely acknowledge that it is absurd to suppose that a rapid itself should have been called ' the Pelican' *on that account;* or, in other words, that it should have been designated in itself as an individual of a certain species of birds characteristic of it. The only circumstance that could give rise to such a designation would be some striking feature in the rapid itself, or the surrounding scenery, bearing a marked resemblance to some characteristic peculiarity of that bird, its beak for instance, or its voracity. Consequently there must, it seems to me, be some error in Constantine's statement as to the name of this rapid. We must necessarily assume one of two alternatives : either there is something wrong in the form of the name handed down to us by him, some derivative termination having been omitted; or the interpretation he gives us of the word is incorrect. If we consider how loose and vague many of Constantine's interpretations of these names are, whereas the names in themselves are fairly correct, I have no doubt that the latter alternative in every respect is the more probable of the two ; especially as pelicans are never even seen there [1]. Constantine who evidently understood something of the Slavonic language may have known that the word *ncyęsyt'* signifies a pelican, and therefore may have added, of his own, the story of the pelicans.

[1] Comp. Lehrberg, l. c., p. 362.

But the Slavonic *neyęsyt'* means more than a pelican. It is a derivative from the adjective *syt'* (сытъ), satiated [1], and the primitive meaning of it is, 'the insatiable;' hence it is used to denote different creatures, especially birds, distinguished by their voracity, for instance, the vulture, or the pelican (in German *Nimmersatt*) [2]. Consequently, according to the primitive meaning of the word, it might very well be the rapid itself that was called 'the Insatiable,' and that this was really the case, is strongly corroborated by the modern name of this rapid, *Nenasytets* or *Nenasytetski*, which is evidently nearly the same as the Old Slavonic name, but which can mean only 'the Insatiable [3].' This is really in itself a very suitable name for such a mighty and violent rapid, and much more significant than the mild term the 'Pelican-fall [4].' Furthermore, I believe it was not so

---

[1] Comp. Fr. Miklosich, Vergleichende Grammatik der Slavischen Sprachen, vol. ii. Stammbildungslehre, p. 374. Wien, 1875.

[2] Old Slavonic *neyęsyt'*, vultur, pelecanus (Miklosich, Lexicon Palaeoslovenico-graeco-latinum. Vindobonae, 1862-65); Russian *nevásyt'* (неясытъ), a pelican? a kind of owl; a fabulous, voracious, insatiable bird; a man insatiably greedy for food, wealth, &c. (Даль, Толковый словарь живаго великорускаго языка. ii. Москва, 1865); Bohemian *nejesyt*, a pelican. Comp. Old Slavonic *nesyt'* (несытъ), pelecanus; Russian *nésyt'* (несытъ), a glutton, an insatiable man or animal; Servian *nesit*, 'Nimmersatt, insatiabilis' (Vuk Steph. Karadschitsch, Lexicon Serbico-germanico-latinum. Vindobonae, 1852); Bohemian *nesyt*, a glutton, a pelican.

[3] Old Slavonic *nenasyt'* (ненасытъ), 'fames'; Russian *nénasyt'* (ненасытъ), a glutton; Servian *nénásit*, 'Nimmersatt, insatiabilis;' Polish *nienasyciec* id.; Bohemian *nenasyt*, a glutton. I add that the only one of the previous interpreters who supports this signification even of the ancient name *Neasit* is Lehrberg (l. c., p. 364). Is perhaps even the form *Neasit* in Constantine a fault instead of *Nenasit*, Νεναστ̄τ?

[4] Compare, for instance, the Old Norse *svelgr*, a swirl, whirlpool,

called from its violence and voracity in general; for
there is a characteristic peculiarity of this very rapid
when compared with the other ones, from which,
it might specially deserve the name 'the Insatiable.'
In the spring, from March to June, the quantity of
water in the river increases so much that the rocks
and stones which are the causes of the rapids are
covered by the water, and in this season therefore
most of the rapids are more or less navigable.
The only exception is the Nenasytets. The obstacles
which here stem the stream and form this rapid
are so enormous that there is never sufficient water
to cover them, and however abundant the supply
of water may be in spring time, its violence is
never diminished [1]. According to Constantine's description this rapid was also the only one in which
the Russ could not even tow their empty boats
through the current, but were obliged to drag them
round it by land. This rapid is consequently like a'
bottomless pit that is never filled, and from this point
of view no name could be more proper for it than
'*Neasit*,' or *Nenasytets*, 'the Insatiable.'

Only after having thus established the true meaning, as I believe, of the Slavonic name shall we be
able to make out the origin and signification of
the Russ name *Aïfar*, of which no satisfactory

current, also as a proper name; a swallower, spendthrift; from the verb
svelgja, to swallow; or *sarpr*, the crop of a bird, hence a renowned waterfall in Norway.

[1] 'Au l'rintemps lors que les neiges fondent, tous les Porouys sont
couuerts d'eau excepté le septième qui s'appelle Nienaslites et qui
seul empesche la nauigation en cette saison.' Beauplan, Description
d'Ukranie, p. 20 (comp. Lehrberg, l. c., p. 321 note).

interpretation has hitherto been suggested [1]. With reference to the pelican theory, the interpreters have generally identified *Aïfar* with the modern Dutch *ooievaar*, Old Low German *ôdebaro*, Frisian *adebar*, a stork; supposing that the Scandinavians who did not know the pelicans in their aboriginal country may have confounded them with storks [2]. But it has been clearly shewn by a Dutch scholar, Prof. M. de Vries [3], that this interpretation is inadmissible as a matter of natural history, the stork being just as much unknown as the pelican in those regions of Scandinavia, from which the immigration to Russia must have taken place: it is also inadmissible on philological grounds; for the word in question is only Low German, not existing in any Scandinavian dialect, and if we reduce it to the language of the tenth century, every resemblance with *Aïfar* vanishes: lastly, it is inadmissible for logical reasons, for it is, and will ever be, absurd to suppose a rapid to have been called ' *the Stork*' or anything of that kind, because pelicans live in the neighbourhood of it [4]. If the interpreta-

---

[1] [Comp. the additions at the end of the book].

[2] Comp. Kunik, Die Berufung der schwed. Rodsen, ii. p. 431 ff, and in Mémoires de l'Acad. Imp. de St. Pétersbourg, viie série, tome xxiii. p. 415. Гротъ (Grot), Филологическія разысканія. 1873, p. 448 ff.

[3] See Verslagen en Mededelingen der koninklijke Akademie van Wetenschappen, Afdeeling Letterkunde, 2de Reeks, Deel V. Amsterdam, 1875.

[4] As to the attempt Prof. de Vries himself makes to explain this name, it is by no means better. He supposes ΑΕΙΦΑΡ to be miswritten for ΔΕΙΦΑΡ, *Difar* (i. e. *Dyfari*) which he compares with the English 'a diver.' But '*dyfari*' is a fictitious word which is just as far from being Scandinavian as *ooievaar* is, and, upon the whole, according to the preceding reasoning I must deem every search in this way to be in the wrong direction.

tion of the Slavonic name *Neasit* which I have given is correct, it must be possible to explain the Russ *Aifar* in harmony with it, and so it is in the most simple and natural manner. In my opinion *Aïfar* represents the Old Norse *Eifari* or *Eyfari* (or *Æfari*), the ever-rushing (perpetuo ruens), the never-ceasing, from *ei-* or *ey-* (or *æ-*), always, ever, and *fari*, a derivative from the verb *fara*, to go on [1]. In the old Swedish of the tenth century the corresponding form would probably be *Aifari* [2]. I believe this interpretation is in all respects satisfactory. You will see that in this way the Russ *Aïfar* gives in the affirmative form ('the ever-rushing'), just the same idea as the Slavonic *Neasit* does in the negative form ('the never-satiated'), and the proposed inter-

---

[1] Compare Old Norse *eimuni, eymuni*, ever-memorable; *eilífr, eylífr, ælífr* (perpetuo vivens), eternal; *eyglò, eyglóa* (perpetuo splendens), the sun; further, with respect to *fari, aynfari* or *gnýfari* (cum strepitu ruens), poetical names of the wind. The compound *eyfari* itself cannot be exemplified from Old Norse literature; but *ey fara* as a verb in the signification 'to go on for ever,' occurs in a verse from the Edda: 'ár of bæði þau (summer and winter?) skulu ey fara, unz rjúfask regin' (Vafþrúðnismál 27. Comp. Norrœn Fornkvæði, almindelig kaldet Sæmundar Edda hins fróða, udgiven af Sophus Bugge, pp. 69 and 396. Christiania, 1867), expressing just the same meaning as Genesis viii. 22: 'While the earth remaineth, . . . summer and winter, and day and night shall *not cease*.'

[2] The Teutonic diphthong *ai*, Old Norse *ei*, seems in Sweden to have conserved for a long time its original form *ai*, and so it is written extremely often in Runic inscriptions (comp. Rydqvist, Svenska Språkets Lagar, vol. iv. p. 138 ff. Stockholm, 1868). Instances where the prefix in question occurs in the form *ai* are AILIFR (Liljegren, Run-Urkunder. Stockholm, 1833, No. 186, 187, 704); AIFIKR (ibid., 489); AIRIKR (ibid., 458, 601, 605, &c.). As to *fari* in Old Swedish, comp. Rydqvist, l. c., vol. ii. p. 183, 1852; it is of frequent occurrence in Old Swedish proper names, as AFARI (Liljegren, l. c., 389); A[S]FARI (ibid., 837) SUFARI (ibid., 702); VIFARI (ibid., 67, 389, 574).

pretations thús mutually corroborate each other; the
name exactly agrees with local nature, and connects
itself naturally and without constraint with the idiom
to which all the other Russ names incontestably
belong.

The name of the fifth rapid is in Russ *Baruforos*,
in Slavonic *Vulniprakh*, and it is said to be so called,
because it forms a large whirlpool ('Ρωσιστὶ μὲν Βαρου-
φόρος, Σκλαβινιστὶ δὲ Βουλνηπράχ, διότι μεγάλην λίμνην
[*leg.* δίνην] ἀποτελεῖ). This name again is one of
the clearest of them all; it means in both languages
'the Wave-fall' or 'Whirl-fall.' The Slavonic form
Vulniprakh represents the old Slavonic *Vl'n'nyi
prag'* (влънъныи прагъ); the word *prag'*, a rapid, we know
already, and *vl'n'nyi* is an adjective derived from *vl'na*,
modern Russian *volná*, a wave, in the same manner
as in the name of the second rapid *ostrov'nyi* was
derived from *ostrov'*, an isle. This rapid is in fact still
called *Volnyi* or *Volninski*[1]. As to the Russ counter-
part of it, *Baruforos*, it is pure Old Norse *Báru-fors*,
a compound of *bára* (genitive case *báru*), a wave, and
fors, a waterfall, which has here been conformed by
the Greek author to the common Greek word -φόρος,
-*phoros*.

The next rapid we come to, the sixth, is said to be
called in Russ *Leanti*, in Slavonic *Verutzi*, which
is interpreted as 'the boiling of the water' (. . . λεγόμενον μὲν 'Ρωσιστὶ Λεάντι, Σκλαβινιστὶ δὲ Βερούτζη, ὅ ἐστι
βράσμα νεροῦ). The literal translation would have
been the boiling or bubbling fall. *Verutzi* is a repre-

[1] Lehrberg, l. c., p. 329.

sentative of the Old Slavonic *v'rashtii* (вър,иштии)[1], a participle of the verb *v'rêti* (върътн), to boil, bubble, also to well, spring forth. The Russ name *Leanti* is evidently a Scandinavian participle like '*Gelandri*,' *Gellandi*, and the comparison which first offers itself is the Old Norse *hlæjandi*, Old Swedish *leiànde* or *leande*, laughing. The designation of a rapid as *the laughing* is in itself by no means unreasonable ; an English audience, I am sure, will instantly think of 'the laughing Water,' Minnehaha, in Longfellow's Hiawatha. According to the signification of the Old Norse verb *hlæja*, to laugh, it may have been so called both from its rippling or babbling sound and from the glittering or sparkling of the foam. In both cases this name may very well correspond with the Slavonic name. I may add that this rapid seems to me to be that which is now called *Tavolzhanski*. The Dnieper is here more than half a mile broad, and filled with stones, a circumstance which may certainly render this rapid peculiarly boiling and foaming, though it is not particularly dangerous.

Finally we have the seventh and last rapid the name of which is said to be in Russ *Struvun*[2], in Slavonic *Naprezi*, signifying 'the small rapid' ('Ρωσιστὶ μὲν Στρούβουν, Σκλαβινιστὶ δὲ Ναπρεζῆ, ὁ ἑρμηνεύεται μικρὸς φραγμός). The explanation of both these names presents great difficulties and has been much disputed. As to the Slavonic name *Naprezi*, none of the hypotheses which have been proposed, appear to be admissible. I rather think that it must be connected

---

[1] Comp. the Servian *vrué*, fervidus.
[2] [Comp. the additions at the end of the book.]

with the Old Slavonic adjective *br's'* (брьзъ), quick,
or some derivative of it, of which several occur in
different Slavonic idioms with the signification of a
small rapid ; thus the Old Slavonic *br'zina* or *br'zhai*,
a current, a stream, 'fluentum,' the Bulgarian *br'ziy*, a
rapid, 'strom-schnelle,' the Servian *brzica* or *brzak*, a
spot in a brook where the water runs rapidly over the
pebbles[1]. I suppose we must think of some word of
this kind, compounded with the preposition *na*, the
meaning of which in this connection this is not the
place to discuss. At any rate, you will see that this
explanation just gives us the signification needed, that
of 'a small rapid.' We must consequently suppose the
Russ name to have a similar meaning. It must
undoubtedly be read *Struvun*, according to the
common signification of the Greek β at that time, not
Strubun as has hitherto been generally assumed. I
think that *Struvun* simply represents the Old Norse
straumr, a stream, current, a word which is not
only extremely often used as a proper name in the
Scandinavian countries, but which also corresponds
very well both to the Slavonic name and to Constantine's translation. This rapid appears to be the same
which is now called *Lishni:* at this point the river is
rather narrow, the greater part of it being occupied
by a large island, but for this very reason it is all the
more rapid ; and as it presents no other danger or
hindrance to navigation, it may very well be called
' the small rapid ' or 'the stream.'

---

[1] For similar names compare Miklosich, Slavische Ortsnamen aus
Appellativen, in Denkschriften der k. k. Akademie zu Wien, vol. xxiii.
p. 149, No. 40.

These are the celebrated names of the Dnieper rapids as they are transmitted to us by Constantine Porphyrogenitus. From the foregoing explanation it will be evident that the so-called Russ names in reality are pure Old Norse or Old Swedish, and these names are therefore without doubt one of the clearest proofs that we possess of the Scandinavian origin of the Russ. The accuracy of this testimony is acknowledged by all, and even the partisans of the various anti-Scandinavian theories have hardly ventured to contest these names, but have avoided them or contented themselves with vague allusions or loose postulates of the most unscientific kind [1].

But though these names of the Dnieper rapids are certainly the only direct specimen we have of the language of the ancient Russ, another group of linguistic mementos has come down to us from them, in which, still more clearly perhaps than in the names of those rapids, we perceive a Scandinavian tongue. I mean the proper names of persons which are to be found in the first pages of Russian history [2]. Not only do these names give us the most decisive proof of the Scandinavian origin of the Russ, but a minute

---

[1] Comp. Kunik in Mémoires de l'Acad. Imp. de St. Pétersbourg, vii* série, tome xxiii. pp. 414, 415.

[2] These names have been treated previously by Bayer in Commentarii Academiae Scient. Imper. Petropolitanae, tom. iv. ad annum 1729, pp. 281-291. St. Petersburg, 1735 (compare A. L. v. Schlözer, Nestor, Russische Annalen, vol. iv. pp. 51-55. Göttingen, 1805). Kunik, Die Berufung der Schwed. Rodsen, vol. ii. pp. 107-194. 1845. P. A. Munch in Samlede Afhandlinger udgivne af G. Storm, vol. ii. pp. 191, 254-256. Christiania, 1874 (1849); and in Chronica Nestoris ed. Fr. Miklosich, pp. 188-198. Vindobonae, 1860. K. Gislason in Nestor's Russiske Krönike oversat af C. W. Smith, pp. 321-326. Kjöbenhavn, 1869.

examination of them will even give us most remarkable information as to the details of this question [1].

We find altogether about ninety names which bear more or less evidence of their Scandinavian origin. Among these names stand in the first place the names of the members of the Russian reigning family in the first two or three generations : *Rurik'* = Old Norse Hrœrekr ; *Sineus'* = Signiutr ; *Truvor'* = Þorvarðr ; *Oleg'*, [*Olg'*] = Helgi ; *Olga* = Helga ; *Igor'* [*Ingor, Inger*] = Ingvarr ; *Malfrid'* = Malmfriðr ; (*Oskold'* = Höskuldr ; *Dir'* = Dýri). Towards the middle of the tenth century they are supplanted by Slavonic names, and after that time a few only of the Scandinavian names continue to be employed in the reigning family as an inheritance from the ancestors (such as *Rurik'*, *Igor'*, *Oleg'*, *Olga*).

But besides these princely persons, almost all the Russian noblemen or private persons who are mentioned in the chronicles, during the first century after the foundation of the Russian state, have pure Scandinavian names. Very few of these names outlive the year 1000. The richest repertories of them are the two treaties concluded between the Russ and the Greeks in the years 912 and 945 [2]. Both of them

---

[1] For all details see the Appendix at the end of this book, where I give a complete alphabetical list of the names in question.

[2] If any one calls the genuineness of these treaties in question, I will answer him with the words of an eminent Slavonist (F. Miklosich, in his edition of Chronica Nestoris, p. ix. s., Vindobonae, 1860) : ‘De foederibus factis cum Graecis confitemur, nos non intelligere, quomodo haec foedera, paucissimis exceptis continentia nonnisi nomina Scandica, fingi potuerint post Nestoris aetatem, Russis tam brevi tempore obiitis haec nomina. Affirmanti vero, ficta esse aut a Nestore aut saltem aetate

begin with the words: 'We of Russian birth,' and thereafter follows a list of the Russian plenipotentiaries. In the first treaty fifteen ambassadors are enumerated; in the latter, probably twenty-five ambassadors, each ·representing some member of the princely family or person of the highest rank, and twenty-five merchants. In the treaty of 912 there are no Slavonic names at all, in that of 945 only three, all belonging to the group of princely persons or noblemen (viz. *Sviatoslav'* son of Igor', *Vladislav'* and a woman *Predslava*)[1]. But there are about sixty names in the treaties, and (exclusive of the princely names) about ten met with elsewhere which incontestably are pure Scandinavian; besides there are some which in all probability are the same (as, for instance, *Aktevu, Istr', Klek', Kuci, Mutur', Sfan'da, Vuzlêb'*), and others which evidently have come down to us in so distorted a form, that it is difficult or impossible at all to trace their origin with certainty (as *Apubksar', Kanitsar', Libi, Sinko Borich', Tilen, Voist' Voikov', Yatviag'*).

It would certainly be impossible to understand how, at those times particularly, non-Scandinavian people should happen to bear names purely Scandinavian, and as the persons who bore those names expressly declare

<hr>

Nestoris, respondebimus, fictionum aetatem in Russia longe esse recenti-orem saeculo duodecimo. Addemus, foedera haec, si quidem ficta sint, ficta esse lingua graeca.'

[1] Among the names which occur without the treaties, and which have been considered as Scandinavian, *Blud'* is pure Slavonic, *Glêb'* originally Bulgarian (see Kunik, Mémoires de l'Acad. Imp. de St. Pétersbourg, vii⁰ série, tome xxiii. p. 402). *Liut'* may be either Scandinavian or Slavonic.

themselves in the treaties to be 'of Russian birth' (*ot'*
roda rus'ska), this is incontestably a most striking
proof that the Russ really were Scandinavians. The
opponents of this view have not been able to shake
this testimony, and will to the end of time be obliged
to renounce all hope of doing so. *T's tour de force*

. But we can go still a step further. It must be remembered that besides a great many names which in
antiquity were nearly equally spread over all the
Scandinavian countries, there are others which were
employed only within more narrow boundaries, and
from such names we can often, with more or less
certainty, draw a conclusion as to the country, sometimes even as to the part of a country, of which the
person who bore it was a native. Those who have
previously examined the Scandinavo-Russian names
have mostly taken into consideration only such names
as are preserved in Old Norse book-literature, which
chiefly concerns Iceland and Norway. However, there
are several of the Russian names which cannot be
thoroughly explained or verified by this means only,
but which nevertheless are clearly Scandinavian in
their roots. But of all the northern countries Sweden
is the one which all the evidence points to as the
chief centre of the relations between Scandinavia and
Russia, and I really think we cast a new light upon
the Russian names, if, instead of confining ourselves
to the Saga-literature, we take for base the names
which occur in the numerous Swedish Runic inscriptions and mediæval papers.

If we follow this plan, we find among the Russian
names a great many which Sweden shares equally

with the other Scandinavian countries. Such names
are *Adulb'* (Auðulfr), *Adun'* (Auðunn), *Akun'*
(Hákun, Hákon), *Aldan'* (Halfdanr), *Alvard'* (Hall-
varðr), *Amun'd'* (Ámundi or Hámundr or Eymundr),
Asmud' (Ásmundr), *Bern'* (Björn), *Budy* (Bóndi), *Dir'*
(Dýri), *Emig'* (Hemingr), *Frelaf'* (Friðleifr, Frilleifr),
Frudi (Fróði), *Fursten'* (Þorsteinn), *Grim'* (Grímr),
Gunar' (Gunnarr), *Ingel'd'* (Ingjaldr), *Ivor'* (Ívarr),
Karl' (Karl), *Karly* (Karli), *Kary* (Kári), *Kol'*
(Kollr), *Oleb'*, *Uleb'* (Óleifr, Ólafr), *Olg'*, *Oleg'* (Helgi),
Olga (Helga), *Rogvolod'* (Ragnvaldr, Rögnvaldr),
Ruald' (Hróaldr), *Ruar'* (Hróarr), *Rulav'* (Hróðleifr,
Hrolleifr), *Riurik'*, *Rurik'* (Hrœrekr), *Sfirk'* (Sverkir),
Stir' (Styrr), *Sven'* (Sveinn), *Truan'* (Þróandr, Þrándr),
Turbern' (Þorbjörn), *Turd'* (Þórðr), *Tury* (Þórir),
Ulb' (?) (Úlfr), *Ustin'* (?) (Eysteinn). But besides these
there are several names which appear to belong exclu-
sively to Sweden (a few of them also to Denmark),
or which, at any rate, are particularly frequent in
Sweden. To this group belong *Ar'fast'* (Arnfastr),
Bruny (Brúni), *Farlof'* (Farulfr), *Fost'* (Fasti), *Frasten'*
(Freysteinn), *Gomol'* (Gamali), *Gudy* (Góði or Guði),
Gunastr' (Gunnfastr), *Igor'* (Ingvarr), *Ingivlad'* (Ingi-
valdr), *Karn'* (Karni), *Mony* (Manni), *Ol'ma* (Holmi?),
Shikh'bern' (Sigbjörn), *Sineus'* (Signiutr), *Sludy* (Slóði),
Stud'k', *Studek* (Stœðingr), *Svenald'* (Sveinaldr), *Tuky*
(Tóki, Túki), *Tulb'* (Þolfr), *Vuyefast'* [or *Buyefast'*]
(Véfastr? [or Bófastr?]); compare also *Shibrid'* = Old
Swedish Sigfriðr, *Turbrid'* = Old Swedish Þorfriðr,
(*Sfirk'* = Old Swedish Sverkir), whereas the Norse-
Icelandic forms are Sigröðr, Þorröðr, (Sörkvir). On the
other hand, there are extremely few of the Russian

names of which I have hitherto found no instance in
Swedish records, while they are well known elsewhere
in Scandinavia; such are *Oskold'* (Höskuldr), *Ver'mud'*
(Vermundr), and the female names *Rognèd'* (Ragnheiðr), and *Malfrid'* (Malmfriðr). But if we consider
how scanty the historical documents of Sweden are, as
compared with those of Norway and Iceland, we are
certainly justified in supposing it a mere chance
that no instance of these names has come down
to us.

But we can proceed still farther ; for the names do
not only betray an intimate relation to Sweden in
general, but especially point to certain parts of it,
namely, the provinces *Upland* (north of the Mælar),
Södermanland (south of it), and *East Gotland* (south
of Södermanland). Not only do all the names occur
just in these three provinces, particularly in Upland,
but several of them even appear to be characteristic
of this very tract, as *Karni* (East Gotland), *Signiutr*
(Upland), *Slöði* (Upland and Södermanland), *Staðingr*
(Upland and East Gotland), perhaps also *Farulfr* and
Sveinaldr (all three provinces). It must not be forgotten, it is true, that by far the greater part (about
three-fourths) of the Swedish Runic inscriptions belong to these three provinces. But this circumstance
does not suffice to explain that remarkable coincidence. At any rate, it is curious that among the
Russian names we do not find a single name which
can be proved to have been characteristic of other
provinces than the three in question, e. g. none of the
numerous names exclusively employed in the island
of Gothland, though this island might be expected to

have been, from ancient times, an intermediate link between Sweden and Russia. We must add that those three provinces are situated along the Swedish shore just opposite the Gulf of Finland, and that the numerous Runic inscriptions in which the relations between Sweden and the East are directly alluded to belong almost exclusively to the same three provinces. After all this we are certainly entitled to assert that the Russian proper names which occur during the first century after the foundation of the Russian state are not only, with extremely few exceptions, of pure Scandinavian origin, but that they also decidedly suggest Sweden, and especially the provinces of Upland, Södermanland, and East Gotland, to have been the original homestead of the so-called Russian tribe.

But it is time we should turn to Scandinavia itself, to see what basis can be found there for the Scandinavian origin of the Russ. And, in truth, though we find no direct account of the foundation of the Russian state, we have such a mass of evidence of the close connection that has existed from time immemorial between Scandinavia and the lands on the other side of the Baltic and the Gulf of Bothnia, that, if only for this reason, the accuracy of Nestor's account seems highly probable.

The earliest evidence in this direction is the fruit of archæological researches. With regard to the most ancient art-periods, the Ages of Stone and Bronze, they are so remote that they are of no essential importance to our subject. Yet we may observe, in passing, that the few relics of the Bronze Age which

have been found on these eastern coasts of the Baltic
are decidedly and exclusively due to occasional intercourse with Scandinavia. Our true interest in this
subject dates from the introduction of iron into the
North : it is in this period that we first find traces of
linguistic records in Scandinavia, the Runic inscriptions, which prove that the population at that time
was of the same race as that which has ever since
inhabited those regions. Even the art-culture of the
first Iron Age, comprising, according to the Danish
archæologists, the period from the commencement of
the Christian era to 450 A. D., had found its way on
a large scale into the countries east of the Baltic.
Many objects have been found there which so closely
correspond with the discoveries made in Scandinavia,
that we are forced to acknowledge that they must
have belonged to the same population, or at least to
one closely akin to it. But the circumstance that these
relics are confined to the tracts of land lying near the
coasts, and that they have no resemblance whatever
to the artistic forms found in the interior of these
countries, proves that the culture of the first Iron Age
was brought there from the west, by emigrants from
Scandinavia [1].

The relics of this Scandinavian art-culture of the
Iron Age are especially found round the Gulf of Finland and along a considerable tract of the western

[1] Comp. Worsaae, La colonisation de la Russie et du Nord Scandi-
nave et leur plus ancien état de civilisation, in Mémoires de la Société
Royale des Antiquaires du Nord, nouv. série, 1873-74 (Copenhague),
p. 154 ff. (= Aarböger for nordisk Oldkyndighed, 1872, p. 388 ff.).
Aspelin, Suomalais-ugrilaisen Muinaistutkinnon Alkeita, p. 136 ff.,
Helsingfors, 1875.

coast of Finland, the native inhabitants of which appear at that time to have been Laplanders (or some other Arctic tribe). The antiquities which have been discovered there are so numerous that there can be no doubt that even in that early period there were many Scandinavian settlements along that coast, extending quite down to the innermost part of the Gulf of Finland.

These archæological results agree most remarkably with a linguistic phenomenon which I have elsewhere discussed[1]. I have proved that the Finnish idioms grouped round the Baltic Sea and its gulfs, at that very time, that is to say during the first centuries of the Christian era, were greatly influenced by the Teutonic tongues; and this in two ways, partly by a Scandinavian idiom closely resembling the language which we meet with in inscriptions of the first Iron Age; and partly by a Gothic idiom, which must have been a little more ancient in form than that known to us from the Gothic translation of the Bible made by Ulfilas in the fourth century, while the Goths inhabited the districts near the Danube. From the multitude and character of the words concerned I have shown that this influence must have been exercised at a time when the Finns were not yet dispersed so widely as they are now, and when they lived in closer union east or south-east of their modern territories, and that the Teutonic tribes of whose languages

---

[1] Vilh. Thomsen, Den Gotiske Sprogklasses Indflydelse på den Finske, Köbenhavn, 1869, translated into German by E. Sievers under the title: Ueber den Einfluss der Germanischen Sprachen auf die Finnisch-Lappischen, Halle, 1870.

fragments have in this way been preserved, must have been settled in the same regions. While this Scandinavian influence reached the Finns from the north-west, the regions round the Gulf of Finland, the Gothic came in from the south-west, the tracts between the Vistula and the Dwina, where we know that the Goths once lived, and where antiquities have been found which can only belong to them; none of these antiquities are of later date than c. 400 A. D., by which time the last of the Goths must have vanished from these districts [1].

The Scandinavian influence also, with respect both to art-culture and to language, seems to diminish or to be completely interrupted towards the end of the fifth century, in order to reappear in new forms some centuries later. This circumstance is certainly connected with the great migrations which at that very time took place in the East, and which not only drove the Slavs westwards, but also caused the Finnish race inhabiting Finland and the Baltic coasts at the present day to immigrate thither from the east or south-east.

About the year 700 or a little later a new epoch begins in the history of Scandinavian civilisation, an epoch which, from an archæological point of view, has been called the second Iron Age. But from that period archæology is no longer our only source of information, and though I willingly allow that it continues to shed valuable light on an infinite number of details of social life in the North, yet the im-

---

[1] Comp. above, p. 4 f., and Worsaae, l. c., p. 167 ff. (= p. 399 ff.).

portance of it is diminished by the abundance of other sources which henceforward afford us an insight into Scandinavian history. It is at this period that the Scandinavians appear for the first time on the stage of universal history, and immediately play a part there, such as they have never played before or since; it is the period of those grand Viking expeditions that made the name of '*Northmen*' known and dreaded on the most distant coasts of Europe.

During the preceding period the inhabitants of the Scandinavian countries had taken but little part in the events which convulsed the greater portion of the European continent. They had had time therefore to form and develope a civilisation of their own, though it may certainly have received many prolific germs from the South. This civilisation, which still did not prevent a considerable rudeness of manners and customs, must have been such as to develope that inflexible energy and vigour, and that taste for adventures which were characteristic of the Viking-time; and as to the art-culture, it gradually attained a remarkable degree of perfection, as is clearly proved by the richly adorned and beautiful weapons, and other antiquities which have been discovered in Scandinavia.

As, however, the Scandinavians were thus shut up for centuries within their own frontiers, such an increase of the population must have gradually taken place as left them at last no other resource but that of sallying forth, sword in hand, to win for themselves a new sphere of action and a new home. A leader for such expeditions was easily found among the many petty kings, whose position was rendered highly unsatisfactory to themselves by the increasing centralisation of political power in the Scandinavian lands.

These were the circumstances which, from the beginning of the ninth century, gave the impulse to the Viking expeditions[1].

How these Northmen thus wandered forth, sometimes when it suited them better, as merchants, but most generally as pirates and plunderers, and how they colonized and even founded kingdoms in several countries in the West, need not to be dwelt on in this place.

What is important for our purpose is the fact that a current, similar to that which first carried the Northmen to Western Europe, bore them at the very same time to the lands beyond the Baltic and the Gulf of Finland, *Austrvegr* (the Eastway) as the ancient Scandinavians called them. While the westward stream flowed principally from Denmark and Norway, the movements to the East issued chiefly from Sweden.

It appears that the migration eastward began somewhat earlier than the other, perhaps even as early as the eighth century ; nor can this surprise us, when we remember that these districts, from still more ancient times, were known to the Scandinavians, frequented by them, and, as it were, homelike to them. Their migrations in this period are a renewal of their

---

[1] The same views of the causes of these expeditions have been stated with great erudition and profoundness by J. Steenstrup in his interesting work Normannerne, vol. i. Indledning i Normannertiden. Copenhagen, 1876, 8vo.

ancient traditions, and the name itself, *Austrvegr*, is an expression of this homelike feeling, as it is quite parallel to *Norvegr* (commonly written *Noregr*, Norway, literally the Northway, *Norðweg* in king Alfred's Orosius), whereas no corresponding name is ever applied to the movement in the opposite direction (*Vestrvíking*).

In the Old Norse Sagas and other documents, we find numerous proofs of the intercourse between Scandinavia and the lands beyond the Baltic[1]. It is true, that we do not there find any direct notice of the foundation of the Russian State; for it was an event which passed comparatively unnoticed in the North, and all the more so, as the central point of the Saga literature, Iceland, was so remote from the scene of this event. But countless are the notices we find of trade and navigation, Viking expeditions, and even emigrations in great masses[2], issuing from Scandinavia, chiefly from Sweden, to the coasts of the Baltic and the Gulf of Finland; and numberless are the passages referring to the visits of Northmen to Russia, and to the intimacy between the Scandinavian and Russian reigning families, which can only be explained by a mutual national relationship.

---

[1] All the notices that the Sagas contain on this question are collected in Antiquités Russes d'après les monuments historiques des Islandais et des anciens Scandinaves, éditées par la Société Royale des Antiquaires du Nord. Copenhague, 1850-52, 2 voll. in folio.

[2] Comp. especially Steenstrup, l. c., p. 194 ff. Still at the present day several tracts of the coasts of Finland and Esthonia have a genuine Swedish population, which must once have immigrated thither from Scandinavia; though no tradition gives us any hint as to the period when this immigration took place.

Many of these notices have a legendary character, and belong almost to mythical times; many, on the other hand, refer to well-known historical personages.

The name by which the Scandinavians designated the Russian dominions, especially the northern part of them, was *Garðar*, the plural of *garðr*, a yard, a stronghold[1], or *Garðaríki*. The localities in Russia, or Garðaríki, which are mentioned in the Sagas are more particularly those grouped nearest round the Gulf of Finland, which were evidently constantly frequented by the Scandinavians. Thus mention is often made of the old commercial town *Aldegjuborg*, the Russian (Old-) Ladoga, standing on the little river Volkhov, at some distance from its fall into lake Ladoga, called by the Scandinavians *Aldegja*. Another town which is extremely often mentioned is Novgorod, which was called by the Scandinavians *Hólmgarðr*, probably because it stood on a holm situated at the point where the Volkhov issues from lake Ilmen[2].

---

[1] This word is akin to the Russian *gorod'*, Old Slavonic *grad'*, a stronghold, a town, which occurs in all Slavonic languages and cannot therefore well be borrowed from the Old Norse *garðr*. I would rather call attention to the fact that the Old Norse names of several towns in the east have the termination *-garðr*, though *garðr* does not in Old Norse signify a town; thus, for instance, *Hólmgarðr*, *Kœnugarðr*. It seems to me not to be unreasonable that the employment of the word *garðr* in these names is an imitation of the Slavonic *gorod'*, *grad'*. In the same way the Old Norse name of Constantinople, *Mikligarðr*, may have been influenced by the Slavonic name of this town, *Tsarigrad'*, 'the Emperor's town.'

[2] Or is *Hólm-* a representative of *Ilmen*, accommodated to the Old Norse *hólmr*? Comp. Müllenhoff in Haupt's Zeitschrift für deutsches Alterthum, vol. xii. p. 346. Similar accommodations of foreign names are extremely frequent in Old Norse.

The Old Norse name of Kiev was *Kænugarðr*[1], Polotsk was called *Palteskja*, &c.

But the Sagas are not the only written memorials that testify to the frequent visits of the Scandinavians to Russia. They are referred to in many of the Runic inscriptions in Sweden, raised to the memory of men who had fallen in the East[2]. Nearly all these monuments are found in the Swedish provinces Upland, Södermanland and East Gotland, and the time from which they date is chiefly the tenth and eleventh centuries. Many of them only say of the deceased, that 'he fell in a battle in the East,' or 'in Gardar,' or 'at Holmgard,' &c.; but there are others which give more detailed information. Thus we have a series of about 20 stones, found in different parts of the above mentioned three provinces, which all refer to one event,—an expedition headed by a leader named Ingvar. On some of them it is said of the deceased: 'he went eastward with Ingvar,' or, 'he fell eastward with Ingvar,' or, 'he commanded a ship in Ingvar's fleet;' one reads: 'he had long been in the East, and fell in the East under Ingvar,' &c. It is evident that all these inscriptions refer to the same enterprise, which must once have been famous,

---

[1] Accommodated to the Old Norse *kæna*, a kind of boat?

[2] No Scandinavian Runic inscription has been discovered in Russia. But this cannot surprise us, nor can it be adduced as a proof against the Scandinavian origin of the Russ. For the Rune-writing in the form characteristic of the later Iron-Age was not generally adopted in Sweden till the tenth century, consequently long after the emigration to Russia had taken place. In honour of the Scandinavians who afterwards found their death in Russia while serving in the Russian army, cenotaphs with inscriptions were erected in their native place.

and in which many Swedes must have participated.
It has been supposed [1] that the Ingvar who is mentioned here, was no other than the Russian prince
called by Nestor, Igor, by Liudprand, Inger, and that
one of his expeditions is referred to. Several circumstances, however, suggest that these inscriptions
must be nearly a century later than Igor's time;
and it is therefore much more probable that Ingvar
was a Swedish prince of that name, surnamed *hinn
viðförli,* 'the far-travelled,' who, according to the
Icelandic 'Annales Regii,' died in the year 1041 [2].

The testimony of the historic records as to the
connection between the Scandinavians and the eastern
lands is supported, in the clearest manner, by archæological discoveries. We see from numerous coins
which have been found in Russia and the North,
that just at the time of the great Viking expeditions
an extremely lively trade existed between Scandinavia, the East and the Byzantine empire. This
intercourse was carried on through the interior of
Russia [3]. Thus in Sweden great quantities of Arabian
coins (nearly 20,000) have been found, which date from
between 698 and 1002, but the far greater part are

---

[1] P. A. Munch, Det norske Folks Historie, i. 2. p. 80. Christiania,
1853. Antiquités de l'Orient, Monuments Runographiques interprétés
par C. C. Rafn, p. ix. Copenhague, 1856.

[2] See Langebek, Scriptores rerum Danicarum, vol. iii. p. 42. Stur-
lunga Saga, edited by G. Vigfusson, vol. ii. p. 353, Oxford, 1876. This
Ingvar is the principal person in a very fabulous Saga: Sagan om
Ingwar Widtfarne och hans son Swen, utgifwen af N. R. Brocman,
Stockholm, 1762, 4to. Published also in Antiquités Russes, vol. ii.
pp. 141–169.

[3] Compare Nestor's statement that even before Rurik's time there
was a passage from the Varangians (i. e. Scandinavians) down the great
Russian rivers to Greece.

from between 880 and 955, the very time when, according to all evidence, the Scandinavian element was playing so important a part in the history of Russia. It seems that from the tenth century, especially, the island of Gothland was the central point of the trade between Scandinavia and the East; for the largest discoveries of coins have been made here (about 13,000). With these Arabian coins were intermixed other foreign coins which must also have been brought there by traders from the East; among them were many Byzantine coins which bear dates of the tenth and eleventh centuries[1].

In Russia, not only have exactly similar coins been found, but also western European coins—chiefly Anglo-Saxon, which must have been taken there by Scandinavians, and which probably have formed part of that Danegeld which England so often had been forced to pay,—as well as weapons and ornaments of a decidedly northern type. Nor is it merely in the Baltic districts that these objects have been discovered, but also farther in the interior of Russia, chiefly in isolated barrows, apparently raised over chiefs[2]. The most remarkable of these objects are the swords, and a kind of buckle of an oval convex form peculiar to the North, and the type presented by them belongs to

[1] Comp. J. J. A. Worsaae, La colonisation de la Russie et du Nord Scandinave et leur plus ancien état de civilisation, in Mémoires de la Société Royale des Antiquaires du Nord, nouvelle série, 1873-74, Copenhague, pp. 190, 191 (= Aarböger for nordisk Oldkyndighed og Historie, 1872, Kjöbenhavn, p. 422 f.).

[2] Comp. Worsaae, l. c., p. 186 ff. (=418 ff.). Comte A. Ouvaroff, Étude sur les peuples primitifs de la Russie. Les Mériens. Traduit par M. F. Malaqué. Pp. 44 ff., 84 ff., 115 ff. &c. St. Pétersbourg, 1875.

the period between the ninth and eleventh centuries;
they correspond exactly to the northern weapons and
ornaments which are found in Great Britain, Ireland,
and France, and date from the time when the Danish
and Norse Vikings visited and settled in those countries,
in other words, from the ninth to the eleventh centuries.
It is to be hoped that, in time, still more light may be
thrown on this subject when such researches in Russia
are carried on with more system, and on a larger
scale than has been the case hitherto.

When we reflect upon the testimony which I have
adduced from Scandinavian documents and archæological discoveries, I think it must be acknowledged
that they support and illustrate, in a most remarkable
manner, the traditional view as to the Scandinavian
origin of the Russ. None of them, it is true, give us
any direct statement of this fact; the greater part of
them refer to the time after the foundation of the
Russian state, and only prove that, at that period,
the Scandinavians carried on a lively intercourse with
Russia, and that a great many of them came over
there, some as merchants, some to serve as warriors
under the Russian princes. But it is evident that
even this intercourse, this influx of Scandinavians into
Russia, would be incredible, had it not for base some
national kinship. I think that even if no other
notice were left to us, we should still be obliged
to suppose the existence of a strong Scandinavian
element in Russia.

But there is another circumstance which, if only
indirectly, yet in a high degree confirms the view
which I am endeavouring to defend. That circum-

stance is the striking resemblance between both the culture and mode of life of the Scandinavians of the Viking times and the ancient Russ, as they are described to us in the Slavonic chronicles, by Greek and Arabian writers. According to the unanimous testimony of these different authorities, the Russ were a seafaring people, a people that wandered far and wide, to Greece and the Oriental lands, and whose ships not only navigated the rivers of Russia, but also the Black Sea, nay, even the Caspian Sea. Everywhere they appear, now as Vikings, now as traders, as it suited them better, but always sword in hand, and ready at any moment to exchange the merchant's peaceful occupation for the bloody deeds of the pirate. This picture of the ancient Russ so completely coincides with the habits and adventurous life of the Northmen, as it is described to us both by northern writers and by the Latin authors of the middle ages, that it is impossible not to believe that these movements issued from the same nation and were inspired with the same national spirit. It is impossible, on the other hand, to imagine this to be the mode of living among the Eastern Slavs of that time. We must remember that they then still dwelt in the interior of the land, completely separated by other tribes from both the Black Sea and the Baltic. How could it then be possible for this people to have become so familiar with navigation as the ancient Russ evidently were[1]? From the first moment this people appears

---

[1] Comp. Kunik in Mémoires de l'Acad. Imp. de St. Pétersbourg, vii⁰ série, tome xxiii. p. 283, and in О записк҇ готскаго топарха, in Записки Имп. Акад. Наукъ, vol. xxiv. p. 110 ff.

upon the stage of history, they prove themselves to
be a maritime nation; such people must previously
have dwelt on the sea coasts, and have been accustomed to manœuvre their ships on the open sea.

If we compare this with the other evidence which
I have previously reviewed, I believe that every
impartial judge will come to the conclusion that
Nestor is perfectly correct in representing the original
Russ as Scandinavians. It is clear that the settlement of the Scandinavian element in Russia, and the
foundation of a Scandinavian state among the Finnish
and Slavonic tribes of that vast territory, was only a
single instance of the same mighty and widespread
movement which in the middle ages carried the
Northmen to Western Europe. A closer consideration
of that part of the question which may still appear
unexplained, I mean the particular name applied to
the Scandinavian element in Russia, and its history,
shall be the subject of the next lecture. I hope, then,
to be able to show that all apparent discrepancies
blend into the simplest and most beautiful harmony.

LECTURE III.

IN the preceding Lecture I reviewed the evidence which can be adduced from other sources to confirm Nestor's account of the foundation of the Russian state, and I think that we have thus obtained a complete corroboration of his statement as to the Scandinavian origin of the ancient Russ. I have referred to some of the arguments used by the anti-Scandinavianists to weaken the power of the different proofs produced by their adversaries; but, on the other hand, I hope I have shown that they are far from having succeeded in their attempts. Especial attention has been called to the linguistical evidence, founded upon the proper names which occur in early Russian history, and upon the few words which have been handed down to us of the language of the ancient Russ (the names of the Dnieper rapids); this evidence seems to be so decisive, that the opponents of the Scandinavian theory have hardly made any serious attempt to gainsay it.

To show the improbability of Nestor's account, the anti-Scandinavianists have taken particular pains to prove the existence of the Russ as a distinct tribe in Russia long before the year stated by Nestor. I have

mentioned the most important of these presumed
proofs, and believe I have shown how untenable they
are : I will only add, that even if such evidence could
be admitted, it would only prove that the date given
by Nestor is incorrect ; while it would not touch the
question of the original nationality of the Russ, a
fact which is independent of chronology, to a certain
extent at any rate.

But the weightiest argument of the anti-Scandinavianists lies in the name *Russ* itself, and it must
be owned that the defenders of the Scandinavian
theory have not hitherto been able to clear up the
difficulties connected with this name. If the Russ
be Scandinavians — thus argue their opponents
— it must be possible from other sources to find
some Scandinavian tribe who called themselves by
that name ; but no such tribe can be indicated.
I willingly acknowledge that this is true, but I
must also observe, that neither is it possible to find
any Slavonic tribe to whom this name originally
belonged ; for the efforts that have been made to prove
this are mere airy conjectures which cannot stand the
test of severe scientific criticism.

But how do we know that the ancient Russ really
called themselves Russ, or anything similar, in their
mother-tongue? Were this clearly proved, the con-
tention of the opponents of the Scandinavian theory
would have real weight ; but in fact there is evidence
which shews that most probably the Old Russ did
not give themselves this name. I therefore consider
it a great mistake on the part of the adherents
of the Scandinavian theory, that they should,

so to speak, waste ·powder and shot in endeavouring to find traces of a Scandinavian or Teutonic
tribe, from whose national appellation the name
Russ might have been directly derived.

The only evidence that may be supposed to
indicate that this name was· a native one, is
the passage from Prudentius which I mentioned
in my preceding Lecture (p. 39); it is also the
earliest authority in which we meet with this name.
My readers will remember that Prudentius relates
how the Greek emperor sent· to Louis the Pious
some ambassadors who had been in Constantinople,
and who, the author adds, rendering the wording
of the Greek letter of introduction, 'said that they,
that is to say, their nation, are called Rhos[1];' but
in Germany these people were discovered to be
Swedes. If we examine the question a little closer,
we shall see that this passage proves nothing. It
is certain that these people could not have treated
with the court in Constantinople in their mother-
tongue, which no one there could understand, nor is it
probable that any of them could speak Greek. The
negotiations therefore must have been carried on by
means of a third language, which both parties mutually
understood, or for which interpreters at least were at
hand. Such a language will probably have been the
Slavonic or Khazarian. At any rate, the name applied

---

[1] What the wording of the Greek original writing was we unfortunately
do not know ; but I think it must doubtless have been something like
τινὰς λεγομένους 'Ρῶς or τινὰς τῶν λεγομένων 'Ρῶς, a very common
expression in Byzantine literature which would very well bear Prudentius'
translation ; if so, it much weakens the argument that those people
called themselves *Russ*.

to these persons at the Greek court must have been
that by which their nation was known in that language
in which they conversed. Let us suppose, by way of
illustration, that a German embassy is sent to an
Indian prince who has never before heard anything of
Germany; the negotiations would naturally be carried
on in English, either directly, or with the assistance of native interpreters; consequently, the nation
to which these ambassadors belonged would be known
in India as 'Germans,' and none would suspect
that in their own language they called themselves
'Deutsche.' If this supposed Indian prince were to
send these persons to some other prince, his letters
of introduction would naturally run as follows: 'The
bearers of these letters are some people who say that
their nation is called "Germans"'—but this would
be no proof that in their own tongue they called themselves so.   Now, if this second prince had not heard
this name 'Germans' before, but, on the contrary, had
known the Germans as 'Deutsche' or 'Allemands,'
he would probably be astonished to find that they
belonged to the nation which he knew so well under
another name: and supposing he had reason to
suspect their intentions, he would possibly act as
Louis the Pious acted.   In short, it does not appear
to me that we can draw the conclusion from this
passage of Prudentius, that the people who were
called *Rhos* by the Greeks, really called themselves
so in their own language.

That they did not we may suppose from the passage of Liudprand, which I have already quoted
(p. 47), in which he says that the people who in

Western Europe were called Northmen, were called by the Greeks 'Rusii [1].'

I therefore boldly venture to maintain that the ancient Russ, taken as a nation, did not call themselves so in their mother-tongue. *Russ* was only a name applied to them in the East. But if this be the case, the objection to their Scandinavian origin, which is founded on the name Russ, is of no importance. It is just as if we would deny that the ancient *Germani* were Germans; for it must now be considered as proved, that no German or Teutonic tribe ever called themselves by that name, but that it was only assigned to them by their Celtic neighbours, and from them was transmitted to the Romans. The same argument would make us deny that the *Wallachians* are of Romanic origin, or the *Welsh* of Celtic origin; for neither of these nations themselves ever knew anything of that name [2]; it originated among the Teutonic peoples, who by *Walh* designated all whose language they did not understand, partly the Celts, partly the

---

[1] Gedeonov says in his Fragments on the Varangian Question, No. X. p. 100 : 'The notice of Liudprand which is so highly appreciated by the Scandinavianists proves but one thing, viz.: that the name Russ was never a native appellation of the Northmen.' I quite agree with Gedeonov in this last conclusion, to a certain extent at least, though by no means in his assertion, that it is the *only* conclusion that can be drawn from Liudprand's words. But when Gedeonov endeavours first to weaken the importance of Liudprand's identification of Rusii and Northmen by the postulate, in itself totally incorrect, that 'Northmen' is a common name which may also include the Slavs, and afterwards draws the conclusion, from the same passage, that none of the Northmen called themselves Russ, I am surprised he does not perceive that in this manner he annihilates his own argument against the Scandinavian origin of the Russ. 'Qui nimium probat nihil probat.'

[2] Comp. Gaston Paris in the Romania i. p. 1 ff.

Romanic nations. Numberless other instances of a similar variety of names can be cited. Even the name *Northmen* was hardly the native appellation of the Scandinavian Vikings who visited the coasts of Western Europe [1].

But while neither the ancient Russ nor any other Scandinavian tribe called themselves *Russ*, attention was called, even in the last century, to a name which is evidently the same word, and which forms its connecting-link with Scandinavia. It is the name given to *Sweden* by all the Finnish tribes grouped round the Gulf of Bothnia and the Baltic. In Finnish it is *Ruotsi* (and *Ruotsalainen*, a Swede), in Esthonian *Rôts* (and *Rôtslanc*), in the language of the Vot (in the government of St. Petersburg near Narva), *Rôtsi* (and *Rôtsalainê*), and in Livonian *Ruotsi* (and *Ruotsli*). Not only must this be the same name as the Slavonic *Rus'*, but it cannot be doubted that the Slavonic name took its origin from the Finnish appellation. It must ber emembered that the Finnish tribes, as we have previously mentioned, completely separated the Slavs from the sea. When the Scandinavians crossed the Baltic, they must first have come in contact with the Finns; but the Slavs could only have become acquainted with them after their passage through the territory of their Finnish neighbours. It is therefore clear that the Finns must have had a name for the Scandinavians before the Slavs had one, and it was therefore extremely natural that the Slavs should give

[1] Comp. J. Steenstrup, Normannerne, vol. i. Indledning i Normar-nertiden, p. 51 f.

them the same name as they heard applied to them
by the Finns.

Several other hypotheses have been made with
reference to the name *Russ*, especially on the side of
the anti-Scandinavian party, which, of course, will not
acknowledge any connection whatever between this
name and the Finnish *Ruotsi*. But none of them will
hold good against scientific criticism. Thus attention has been called to the Biblical name *Rosh* ('Ρώς
in the Septuagint), which we find in Ezekiel, xxxviii.
2, 3, and xxxix. 1. 'The prince of Rosh, Meshech and
Tubal [1]' is there given as the title of Gog who is
to come up from the north against the people of
Israel, but God will judge him and give the victory
to Israel. It has long ago been objected that this
comparison has no value at all, because the name
Rosh in Ezekiel is too uncertain and solitary, and
between his time and the Russ of the ninth century
there is a space of more than 1400 years [2]. Neverthe-

---

[1] In the English authorised version this name *Rosh* is not to be
found. There this passage is rendered 'the chief prince of Meshech
and Tubal,' like the Vulgate 'principem capitis Mosoch et Thubal,'
according to the common signification of the Hebrew word ראשׁ *rosh*,
which is a head or chief. It is not however improbable that *Rosh* may
be used here to denote some nation or tribe, but certainly not the Russ.
Compare Сказанія еврейскихъ писателей о Хазарахъ. Собралъ А. Я.
Гаркави. Санктпет⁀. 1874, pp. 60 ff., 158 f. Lenormant, Lettres Assyrio-
logiques, vol. i. p. 27, Paris, 1871, connects *Rosh* with the Assyrian
Rashi, 'pays situé sur la rive gauche du Tigre, au nord de la Susiane.
Compare G. Maspéro, Histoire ancienne des peuples de l'Orient, 2⁰ éd.,
p. 402, Paris, 1876: '*Rasi*, canton de la Susiane, la Mésobatère des
géographes classiques.'

[2] So already, Müller, Sammlung Russischer Geschichte, vol. v. p.
390 f. St. Petersburg, 1760 (=vol. ii. p. 343 f. Offenbach am
Main, 1777).

less there are visionaries who even at the present day
seriously quote this text to prove the antiquity of the
Russ.

Next, the name Russ has been connected with the
name *Roxolani*, a 'Sarmatian' tribe that in ancient
times dwelt in some part of what is now Southern
Russia. Some have supposed them to be Slavs or
half-Slavs [1], others have thought that they may have
been Goths [2], or even Scandinavians who had remained
in Russia when their kinsmen, according to an untenable theory, had immigrated into the northern
countries from the East [3]. There can be no doubt,
however, that these Roxolani were of Oriental descent,
probably an Iranic tribe: like so many other tribes
they were swallowed up by the waves of the great
migration, and have nothing to do with the Russ,
whatever origin we may ascribe to them.

It seems to me to be incontestable that the only
name with which the word *Russ* has any direct connection is the Finnish appellation of Sweden, *Ruotsi*,
and this fact is in itself highly instructive with respect
to the question of the nationality of the Russ.
Whence the name *Ruotsi*, in its turn, is derived, is
again a subject of dispute among philologers. The

---

[1] Comp. e.g. the Athenæum, 1872, July 27, p. 113. A Slavonic
root *rus, ros, ras, ra*, referred to, ibid., with the meaning ' river,' does not
exist; see Miklosich, Die Rusalien, p. 19 (in Sitzungsberichte der
phil.-hist. Classe der Kais. Akademie, vol. xlvi. Wien, 1864).

[2] E. g. Müller, Sammlung Russischer Geschichte, vol. v. 1760,
p. 385 ff. (= vol. ii. 1777, p. 339 ff.).

[3] P. A. Munch, Samlede Afhandlinger udgivne af G. Storm, vol. ii.
p. 196 ff. Christiania, 1874 (written 1849). Afterwards, however, he
modified his opinion upon the Roxolani; see his Det Norske Folks
Historie, part I. vol. i. p. 41. Christiania, 1852.

explanation of this word, which has been most generally adopted by the so-called Scandinavian school, is to derive it from *Roslagen*, the name of the coast of the Swedish province of Upland, lying just opposite the Gulf of Finland. Several objections, however, have been raised against the identification of these two words. On the one hand, the first syllable of *Roslagen*, which alone is supposed to have been transferred to the Finnish, is in itself no nominative, but the genitive case of an Old Swedish substantive, *roþ-er* (*rod*, Old Norse *róðr*), rowing, navigation. On the other hand, the name *Roslagen* is too modern to be worthy of consideration; in more ancient times the word *Roþer*, *Roþin* was used to denote those tracts of Upland and East Gotland that bordered the sea, and in the middle ages were bound to furnish ships in time of war. The inhabitants of this district were called *Rods-karlar* or *Rods-mæn* (their modern appellation is *Rospiggar*)[1]. On account of these difficulties this etymology has been since abandoned, even by Kunik who in his work ' Die Berufung der Schwedischen Rodsen,' had supported it with great power[2].

I allow that it is impossible to suppose any direct

---

[1] Comp. Rydqvist, Svenska Språkets Lagar, vol. ii. pp. 273, 628. Stockholm, 1857.

[2] Kunik has lately proposed another explanation (Mémoires de l'Académie Imp. de St. Pétersbourg, viiᵉ série, tome xxiii. p. 381 ff.), connecting the names *Ruotsi* and *Rus* with an Old Norse name *Reiðgotar* or *Hreiðgotar* (in Anglo-Saxon *Hréðgotan* or *Rædgota*), which seems to mean the Goths on the continent; he thinks that the original form of this name may have been *Hróþigutans*. But this explanation is fraught with such great difficulties in its phonetic aspect, that it must be considered untenable.

genetic connection between Roslagen, as a geographical notion, and Ruotsi or Russ. Nevertheless I
have some doubt whether this thread has not been
too precipitately cut asunder. The name *Ruotsi* can
no more be explained from the Finnish language than
Rus' can from the Slavonic. It must therefore be of
foreign, in all probability of Scandinavian origin[1]. But
if it be so, it appears to me by no means unreasonable
to fix upon the Old Swedish word *roþ-er*, all the
more as it is in truth a remarkable coincidence that,
in ancient times, *Roþer, Roþin*, was the name of the
very same tracts of Sweden to which the Russian
personal names, as we have seen before, point as the
original homestead of the Russ. We can easily imagine that the Swedes who lived near the coast and
crossed to the other side of the Baltic, might very
early call themselves—not considered as a nation, but
after their occupation or mode of living—*röps-menn* or
röps-karlar or something similar, i. e. according to the
original signification of the word, rowers, seafarers[2].
In Sweden itself this word, and even the abstract
substantive *roþer*, gradually came to be treated as
proper names. It is then all the less strange that the
Finns should have understood this name to be the
title of the nation, and adopted it in this signification,

---

[1] In a similar manner the Laplanders have derived the words *Ladde*,
1. a (Swedish) village, 2. Sweden; and *Laddelaš*, 1. a (Swedish)
peasant, 2. a Swede, from the Swedish word *land*, land, country.

[2] In Northern Norway *Róssfolk* (*Rórs-* or *Róds-folk*) still signifies
' fishers that assemble near the shore during the fishing time.' The singular form is *Róss-kar* or *-man*. See Ivar Aasen, Norsk Ordbog, p. 612.
Christiania, 1873.

so that they preserved the first syllable only of the compound word, in the forms *Ruotsi* and *Ruotsa-lainen.* It might be objected, as has been done with regard to the derivation from *Roslagen*, that the first syllable of the compound word, *Rōþs-*, is in Swedish a genitive, and that it would be singular to use a genitive form as a proper name. But if we suppose that no Scandinavian called himself *Rōþs* or *Ruotsi* or *Russ*, but that this abridged name was first assigned to them by the Finns, this difficulty vanishes. For it is very common in Finnish, when a compound word is adopted from another language, to keep only the first part of it [1]; and if this first part happen to be originally a genitive, a word may unconsciously be adopted in its genitive form. This is the case, for instance, with the Finnish word *riksi*, a Swedish rix-dollar, which has been formed from the Swedish word *riks-daler* by dropping the principal word *daler* or dollar and only retaining *riks-*, which is originally the Swedish genitive form (for *rikes*) of *rike*, a kingdom [2]. Such an explanation of the Finnish *Ruotsi* I think by no means an unreasonable one. It is only an hypothesis; but it seems to me that this hypothesis in every respect affords clear harmony and coherence.

---

[1] The same sometimes occurs in indigenous words; see A. Ahlqvist, Auszüge aus einer neuen Grammatik der finnischen Sprache. Zweites Stück: Zusammensetzung des Nomens, § 14. Helsingfors, 1872. (Acta Societatis Scientiarum Fennicae, tom. x.)

[2] I will add that, from its form, the Finnish *Ruotsi* may date from the beginning of the so-called second iron-age, or a little earlier; at any rate it must be younger than the first iron-age (compare above, p. 75 f.). See V. Thomsen, Den Gotiske Sprogklasses Indflydelse på den Finske, pp. 70 f., 100 f. Kübenhavn, 1869.

As before said, the same name came from the
Finns to the Slavs in the form *Rus'* (Роусь, Русь),
where the sound *uo* or *ô*, which is unknown in Slavonic, is rendered by *u*, exactly in the same manner
as the Finnish *Suomi*—originally the name of some
Finnish tribe, and now the native name for Finland—is rendered *Sum'* (Соумь, Сумь) in the Russian
chronicles.

As far as the grammatical form of the name *Rus'*
in Slavonic is concerned, it is characteristic that this
word is always used in the singular number as a
collective noun.   Otherwise this peculiarity only
occurs, in Russian documents, in the case of foreign
names, particularly such as designate Finnish tribes or
are derived from the Finnish languages, in which
we really find the model of this usage.   Thus
we have in the Russian chronicles, besides the word
Sum' already mentioned, *Yam'* = Finnish *Häme* (the
Tavastrians), *Mordva*, *Meria*, *Muroma*, *Ves'*, *Chud'*,
Perm', &c. This fact also corroborates our supposition
that the name *Rus'* may have come to the Slavs from
the Finns.

From the Slavonic name *Rus'* is derived the Greek
form of the same word, *Rhôs* ('Ρῶs), which we meet
with in the ninth and tenth centuries.   There may
be doubts as to whether the Greeks received this
form directly from the Slavs (or, which amounts to
the same thing, from the Russ themselves, inasmuch as they used the Slavonic language), or if the
word was transmitted mediately through another language which had previously acquired it from the
same source.   Two things are remarkable in this

Greek form, _Rhôs:_ firstly, the vowel _ô_ (ω), instead of which we should expect _u_ (ου), if the word were derived directly from the Slavonic; next, the peculiarity that it is always used indeclinably in this form, being treated as a plural noun (οἱ 'Ρῶς, τῶν 'Ρῶς, &c.). This latter circumstance can scarcely be sufficiently explained by the constant use of the name _Rus'_ in the singular in Slavonic. I am rather inclined to regard it as suggesting that the first knowledge of this name reached the Greeks through the language of some Turkish-Tatar tribe, probably the Khazars (compare above, p. 42), and that, in the beginning, the Greeks themselves confounded the Russ with those tribes. In Byzantine literature we commonly find Turkish - Tatar names, and those only, used indeclinably in the same way, e.g. οἱ Οὐάρ, Χουννί, 'Ογώρ, Οὔζ, Ταρνιάχ, &c.[1] The same circumstance may possibly explain also the ω of the Greek form Rhos (compare the Hungarian form _Orosz_, Russian, which from the prefixed _o_ is incontestably proved to have been introduced through some Turkish dialect). From about the middle of the tenth century the Greek form Rhos was supplanted by the more modern form _Rusioi_ ('Ρούσιοι), which has more affinity with the Slavonic _Rus'_.

The Arabs received their _Rûs_ in much the same way as the Greeks (or perhaps from the Greek _Rhôs_?).

To the people of Western Europe, especially the

---

[1] Kunik (Mémoires de l'Acad. Imp. de St. Pétersbourg, série vii, tome xxiii. p. 404) explains this use from an identification of the name _Rhos_ with the Biblical 'Ρώς (see above, p. 93). But as early as 839 such an association of ideas seems to me highly improbable.

Teutonic race, this name came later, with the politico-geographical signification in which we now employ the word Russia. In the eleventh century we meet with the Old German form *Rûsâ*, and in mediæval Latin documents we find *Russia, Ruzzia, Rucia,* &c. The Middle High German form is *Riuze.* The name came back to Scandinavia from Germany; in the later Norse Sagas we find *Rûssar* (Russians) and *Rûzaland* or *Rûciland* instead of the more ancient *GarÐaríki,* and in Old Swedish *Ryza,* Russians, *Ryzaland,* Russia, where the vowel *y* (=original *û*), as well as the *z,* a letter foreign to the Swedish language, clearly indicate its German origin[1].

This is in abstract the development of the name Russ regarded from the linguistic side. As to the ethnographical meaning of this name, we have already seen that the Slavs especially used it to denote the Scandinavian tribe which founded a state among them, while the Greeks and Arabs in the ninth and tenth centuries employed it also in a more extensive sense, answering to that of the name Northmen in Western Europe (pp. 49, 50). Now the question arises: What Scandinavian tribe was it to which the Slavs applied the name *Rus'?* And how is it possible for this name to have totally changed its meaning in the course of time and have come to signify a Slavonic nationality instead of a Scandinavian one?

I have before shown how antiquarian discoveries, linguistic evidence, and direct historic records all

---

[1] Comp. Rydqvist, Svenska Språkets Lagar, vol. iv. p. 306.

alike prove that, from time immemorial, there was an extremely lively movement from Sweden to the lands on the other side of the Baltic. After having been interrupted or only continued on a smaller scale for several centuries, this movement was resumed with redoubled energy in the eighth century, and certainly was not then restricted to mere occasional visits of Northmen, but Scandinavian settlers must have established themselves on different parts of the coasts. It must have been these very invaders and settlers to whom the Finns, the native inhabitants of these districts, gave the name *Ruotsi, Ruotsalaiset,* and the Slavs after their example the name *Rus',* whatever the origin and primitive signification of this name may be. At that time neither the Finns nor the Slavs were seafarers, and therefore they could only become acquainted with the Scandinavians when the latter came over to their country. Later on, when the Finns came into closer connection with Sweden, they transferred the name *Ruotsi* to that country itself, while the Slavs, as we shall presently see, acquired in another way a name for the inhabitants of Sweden. It is possible that the *Rhos* who came to Constantinople in 838 or 839 belonged to some such colony, and not to Sweden itself; and the statement we find in certain Mahomedan authors, that the *Rûs* dwelt on an unhealthy island in a lake, may also originally refer to some such settlements.

If we keep this in mind I believe we shall better understand the chief event which Nestor places in 862, the foundation of the Russian state.

In Nestor's account of this event, the source of

which must be the tradition at Kiev, there is one
point that all certainly agree to consider as incorrect.
That is the chronology. But tradition does not care for
chronology, and the date fixed by the chronicles for
this event, 862, can only have been obtained by some
kind of calculations. Nestor refers to this year a
series of events for which it is impossible to find
room in that space of time. According to him, in
this same year the Varangian Vikings were driven
back beyond the sea; the native tribes quarrelled for
some time with each other; the Russ were called in
from beyond the sea; Rurik's two brothers died 'after
the lapse of two years'(!); and two of his followers,
Askold and Dir, mastered Kiev. It is evident that all
this cannot have taken place in one year, but that
here different events are mingled together, which in
reality were separated by a considerable interval, and
862 is probably only the date of the last of them,
the occupation of Kiev. And how is it possible that
in the same year in which the native Finnish and
Slavonic tribes freed themselves from the oppression
of the Varangians, they should, of their own own
accord, have again called in a Varangian clan from
beyond the sea? Here also we must, I am sure,
distinguish different events which the tradition has
combined into one.

In itself it is very improbable that the contending
tribes should have absolutely called in a foreign race
of princes. This point has a somewhat legendary
look. In this respect the remarkable resemblance
between Nestor's account and the relation of the
arrival of the Saxons in Britain is worth noticing.

In his Saxon chronicle Widukind tells us how ambassadors from the Britons addressed themselves to
the Saxons on the continent, and invited them to
help them and rule over them, in almost the same
words which Nestor puts into the mouth of the Slavs
and Finns :—'We offer this our land, which is large
and spacious and abounds in all things, to be at your
command [1].' However, this legend is perhaps only a
naïve, as it were a dramatised, representation of the
fact that the Slavs voluntarily subjected themselves
to the dominion of the Russ. But even if it be so,
the tradition decidedly suggests a difference between
the Vikings who had just been driven away, and the
Russ; the latter must have been a tribe whom the
Slavs were previously acquainted and familiar with.

Thus we are again led to the same result as before.
The Scandinavian clan which the Slavs called especially by the name given to them by the Finns, *Rus'*
(as others are called *Svie*, others *Nurmane*, &c., adds
Nestor), and which about the middle of the ninth
century obtained the mastery over the Slavs, cannot
under any circumstance have been called in directly
by the Slavs from Sweden for this purpose. It must
have been Swedish settlers whose primitive homestead was the coast just opposite the Gulf of Finland,
but who had already for some time lived somewhere
in the neighbourhood of the Finns and Slavs, probably near Lake Ladoga. We may perhaps find

---

[1] 'Terram latam et spatiosam et omnium rerum copia refertam vestrae
mandant ditioni parere.' Widukind, Res gestae Saxonicae. i. c. 8, in
Pertz, Monumenta Germ. hist., Script., vol. iii. p. 419. Comp. Kunik
in Mémoires de l'Académie Imp. des Sciences de St. Pétersbourg, vii.
série, tome xxiii. p. 242 ff.

a reminiscence of such an intermediate settlement
in the notice preserved by some of the Russian
chronicles, that Rurik and his brothers founded the
town of Ladoga (comp. p. 13 note 2) and first settled
there ; for Ladoga really lies outside the ancient
territory of the Slavs.

The mastery of the Russ over the Slavs begins
with their settlement at Novgorod. Their absolute
dominion here did not however attain any stability,
and Novgorod soon ceased to be their capital. The
real foundation of a Russian state dates from the
occupation of Kiev. We have seen that shortly after
Rurik had taken possession of Novgorod, two of his
followers, Askold and Dir, left him and established
themselves there (862 A. D. ?), and in 882 Rurik's
successor Oleg himself seized the town of Kiev and
made it his capital. From this time the name Russ
vanished from Novgorod, and was connected exclusively with Kiev. From this centre it spread itself
in wider and wider circles over all the territory which
has gradually been acquired by the Russian crown.

But as the name *Russians* thus diffused itself, its
signification changed completely. It was once the
ancient Slavonic appellation of the Northmen, and has
at last come to signify a purely Slavonic nationality.

This change is similar to that which has taken place
with respect to the name *Franks* and *France*. As is
well known, the Franks were at first a Germanic tribe
which made themselves masters of Gaul. From this
name, Franks, was formed the name *France* (*Francia*),
a political appellation of the land and the people
that composed the state formerly established by the

Franks, or rather its nucleus the 'Isle de France.' When at last the Frankish nationality had died out or had been absorbed in the far more extensive Romance element, and the various races became blended, nationally as well as politically, the appellation *France, Français, French*, became the name of the united nation, but of quite another nation than that to which it first belonged. A similar instance may be found in the names *Northmen (Normanni)— Normandy—Normans*, and many others.

The evolution of the name *Rus'* or *Russ* was exactly similar. It also was at first the appellation of a foreign Scandinavian clan that gained the mastery over the native Slavonic tribes, though the invaders were of course far inferior to them in number. The name of this tribe, *Rus'*, was then naturally trans-ferred, as a politico-geographical appellation, to all land under the rule of the Russ who dwelt at Kiev (= *rus'skaya zemlia*, the Russian land), next to the inhabitants also, Slavs as well as Northmen, and in this latter signification it gradually superseded the old names of the separate Slavonic tribes. When at last the political union turned into a national unity, the name *Russia, Russians* came of course to denote the whole nation.

This evolution of the name we can distinctly trace in Nestor's account. While he expressly says that the name *Russ* at first belonged to a Scandinavian clan, and he often uses it in this signification, it is obvious that in his own time it had lost this its original signification. He uses it chiefly as the politico-geographical denomination of Kiev and its dominions. In this sense he speaks of 'the Poliane who are now called Russ,' and classes himself among the Russ ('we Russ'); but he ordinarily calls his own nationality and his own language Slavonic, not Russian. However, we see the germ of the modern signification in such phrases as this: 'The Slavonic and the Russian nation' (literally, 'language') 'is one; for they have called themselves Russ from the Varangians, but previously they were Slavonians.'

We have now treated of the origin and history of the name Russ. But there is another name which in Russian chronicles is so closely connected with it that it will be necessary for us to dwell a little upon it. I mean the name *Varangians.*

We have seen that in several passages, for instance that just mentioned, or where Nestor speaks of the foundation of the Russian state, the Russ are identified with the Varangians, or rather are described as a subdivision of the Varangians. It is impossible, in this connection, to give the word Varangians any other signification than Scandinavians. But, as the anti-Scandinavianists have remarked on good grounds, it appears that in other parts of the Russian chronicles a distinction is always made between these two names. In speaking, for instance, of the expeditions of Oleg and Igor, both the Russ and Varangians, as well as Polians, Slavonians, &c., are mentioned as forming part of the armies, and consequently these names must denote two separate tribes. This use of the word has been adduced as evidence against the Scandinavian origin of the Russ, and there is really here an apparent difficulty which has not hitherto, I think, been satisfactorily explained. We must therefore more exactly consider the signification and history of the name Varangians, and try to define the mutual relationship between this name and the name Russ.

That the name Varangians is not confined to Russia alone has long since been observed, and it has been remarked that in Constantinople we meet with the same name, *Warings* or *Varangians* (Βάραγγοι), as the appellation of a body of guards specially consisting of Scandinavians, and in the Old Norse Sagas often mentioned under the name *Væringjar*. In Byzantine writings this body of Warings is mentioned for the first time under the date of 1034[1]. It must however have existed some time before that date, perhaps nearly a century earlier, as we may infer from other documents, Latin and Scandinavian, which allude to them. The first instances we find in the Sagas of Scandinavians expressly mentioned as having served in the Greek army are those of the Icelanders Thorkel Thjóstarsson and Eyvind Bjarnason (in Hrafnkels-saga), both before 950. Next, mention is made in Sagas of Grís Sæmingsson (c. 970–980), Kolskegg Hámundsson (c. 992), and Bolli Bollason (c. 1026–1030)[2]. These however appear to be the only instances at such an early date, as far as Norway and Iceland are concerned at least. The Swedes, on the contrary, may even at that period have furnished the chief contingents to the Varangian body, though

[1] Georg. Cedrenus, p. 735.

[2] See G. Vigfusson, Um timatal í Íslendinga sögum, in Safn til sögu Íslands ok Íslenzkra bókmenta, vol. i. p. 407. Kaupmannahöfn, 1856. Comp. Kunik in Mémoires de l'Acad. Imp. de St. Pétb., vii. série, tome xxiii. p. 35.

the Sagas of course do not mention it[1]. During the
eleventh century, from c. 1030, it became the fashion
for Northmen of rank to take service under the
Greek Emperors, and particularly after ~~that~~ the Norwegian prince Harald Hardrada (who afterwards fell
fighting against Harold the Saxon) had fought
under the Byzantine flag; but after that time also
the bulk of them must undoubtedly have continued
to be Swedes[2]. From that time the Varangian body
formed a *corps d'élite* in the Greek army, to whom
the care of the Emperor's person was specially con-
fided. In this quality they are extremely often mentioned both in Greek and Scandinavian documents,
the former often also alluding to their characteristic
weapon, a long two-edged axe[3]. We do not however
find them only in immediate attendance as the
Emperor's body-guard, but also quartered in other
places[4]. There still exists, at the present day, a
remarkable monument which palpably reminds us
of these Varangians. I mean the colossal marble
lion in a sitting posture which now adorns the
entrance to the Arsenal at Venice. This lion was
brought thither from Piræus after the capture of
Athens by the Venetian general Francesco Morosini
in 1687. From time immemorial this monument had

---

[1] Comp. Kunik, l.c., p. 378.

[2] Compare Cronholm, Wäringarna, pp. 26, 29. Lund, 1832.

[3] From this weapon we often find them expressly designated, especially
by affected authors who shrink from using the vulgar and barbaric name
Varangians, οἱ πελεκυφόροι βάρβαροι, οἱ πελεκυφόροι βασιλέων φύλακες, οἱ
πελεκύν τινα ἐπ' ὤμων φέροντες, οἱ πελέκεις ἔχοντες Βάραγγοι, κ.τ.λ.

[4] Joh. Scylitzes (p. 864), for instance, mentions οἱ ἐκτὸς Βάραγγοι in
opposition to οἱ ἐν τῷ παλατίῳ Βάραγγοι.

stood near the harbour of Piræus, which had taken
from it its Italian name of 'Porto Leone.' It is, in
truth, a work of the best period of ancient Greek
art; but what is most interesting to us is that on it
there is a long Runic inscription, cut in serpentine
curves on both sides of the body of the lion. Un-
happily this inscription is so effaced by time and
weather that it is now almost illegible[1]. From the
form of the serpentine curves and the separate runes,
however, the eminent runologist Professor S. Bugge, in
Christiania, has proved[2] that it was cut, about the
middle of the eleventh century, by a man from
Sweden proper ('Svealand'), probably from the province of Upland; and there can be no doubt that this
man once served among the Varangians and happened
to be quartered at Piræus.

Towards the end of the eleventh century the
Varangian body seems to have begun to change its
character. From that time it was not only recruited
from Scandinavia, but also by Englishmen, who after
the Norman conquest, being driven away from their
native land, or dissatisfied with the state of things
there, repaired to Constantinople to win laurels in
the Greek service: it can scarcely be doubted that
among these Englishmen there were several Danes.
Towards the end of the twelfth century we read in
several authors that the Varangians were Britons

---

[1] The late Danish archæologist C. C. Rafn made an attempt to read
and explain the whole of it (Inscription runique du Pirée = Antiquités de
l'Orient. Copenhague, 1856); but the result must be considered a failure.

[2] In Kongl. Vitterhets Historie och Antiqvitets Akademiens Månads-
blad (Stockholm), No. 43, 1875, p. 97 ff.

(Βρεταννοί), or Englishmen (Ἴγγλινοι), and that they
spoke English (ἰγκλινιστί)[1]. From the beginning of
the thirteenth century the visits of Scandinavians·
to Constantinople became more and more rare[2], and .
finally the Varangian body consisted exclusively of
Englishmen. In this form it seems to have existed
till the fall of the Byzantine empire.

On account of the position of the Varangians at
Constantinople, as well as their frequent appearance
in Russian history as hired troops in immediate
attendance of the princes, this name has hitherto
been unanimously considered as at first designating
a military body, and it has been generally believed
to have originated in Constantinople. It has then
been supposed that only in later times did it come
to signify the nation from which the body-guard
was formed.

From the form of the word *Varangian* or *Waring*
there can be no doubt it is of Scandinavian origin ;
the termination *-ing, -eng, -ang* is neither Slavonic
nor Greek, but Scandinavian[3], and all the interpretations that have not been founded on this supposition
have completely failed. Of the many etymologies

---

[1] Gaufredus Malaterra in his Historia Sicula, lib. iii. c. 27 (Muratori, Rerum Italicarum Scriptores, vol. v. p. 584, 1724), mentions ' Angli
quos Varingos appellant' as forming part of the Greek army in 1081.

[2] Saxo Grammaticus (c. 1200 A.D.) still says : 'Inter caeteros qui Con-
stantinopolitanae urbis stipendia merentur, Danicae vocis homines primum
militiae gradum obtinent, eorumque custodia rex salutem suam vallare
consuevit ' (Saxonis Grammatici Historia Danica, recc. P. E. Müller et
J. M. Velschow, part i. vol. ii, p. 610. Havniae, 1839).

[3] Comp. Miklosich, Die Fremdwörter in den Slavischen Sprachen
(Denkschriften der philosoph.-histor. Classe der kais. Akademie der
Wissenschaften, xv), p. 14. Wien, 1867.

which have been proposed for this word, the only
one that satisfies the requirements of the science of
language is its derivation from the Old Norse *vár*,
usually plural *várar*, a pledge, troth ; in Anglo-Saxon
we find the same word in the form *wǽr*, with nearly
the same meaning—a caution, pledge, covenant.
Thence the word Warings or Varangians has been
supposed to signify 'confederates,' or a body of
'sworn men.' When this interpretation was for the
first time proposed, a foundation for it was supposed
to be found in a still more ancient name *Foederati*
(Φοιδεράτοι)[1], the designation of a body of mercenaries
in the Byzantine army, originally (in the third and
fourth centuries) consisting of Goths, and the Varangian body was believed to be a continuation of
the *Foederati*, so that *Varangian, Waring* would be
the national Teutonic appellation of the same body.
It cannot however be doubted that there was no
continuity or relationship whatever between these
two bodies, as even in the fifth century the Foederati
consisted of the most heterogeneous elements, chiefly
recruited from Oriental nations, and in this form it
seems to have continued to exist contemporaneously
with the Varangians. But if that be the case, there
is good reason to inquire whether the evolution of this
word may not have been quite different from all that
has been assumed hitherto, and all the more as the
Old Norse word *vár-ar*, to which it is referred, is
never used to signify a military oath or an oath of
allegiance.

[1] J. Ihre, Glossarium Suiogothicum, vol. ii. pp. 1069, 1070. Upsaliae,
1769, fol.

Is it really certain that *Varangian* was at first
the designation of a military body, or any military
institution whatever? I do not think so, and must
consider such an opinion to be a mere assumption.
On the contrary, I maintain that the proper signification of the word *Varangian* in the whole of
the East was a distinctly geographical one, viz. that
of Scandinavians, and more particularly Swedes.

When we refer to the Russian chronicles, we always
find the word Varangian (in Russian *Variag'*, plural
Variazi) used in this sense; as, for instance, in that
passage in which the foundation of the Russian state
is spoken of, and in which it is distinctly said that
'some of the Varangians were called Russ, just as
others are called Svie, others Nurmane,' &c.; and
there are numerous other passages which are equally
evident. In short, there can be no doubt that
whether the Varangians are mentioned in Russian
documents as mercenaries in the Russian army, as
is commonly the case in the earlier times, or as
peaceful merchants, which is almost the rule in the
twelfth and thirteenth centuries, the word never
signifies any but Scandinavians, especially Swedes.
This geographical interpretation is the only one which
is satisfactory in every passage. One circumstance
which must assign considerable antiquity to this
signification is that in the chronicles the Baltic Sea
is called 'the Varangian Sea' (*variazh'skoye more*).
That this use of the word was not forgotten
even after the lapse of centuries is clearly proved,
for instance, by the letter which the Russian Czar
Ivan the Terrible wrote to the Swedish king John

the Third in 1573, when he laid claim to the crown
of Sweden. We there find this expression used:
'Your people have served my ancestors from very
remote times; in the ancient annals Variags are
mentioned who were to be found in the Autocrator
Yaroslav-Georgi's army; but the Variags were
Swedes, consequently his subjects[1].' Also in an
account of the siege of the Tikhvin monastery by
the Swedes in 1613, we find them called *Variags*[2].

If we turn to the Arabic writers we find there also
the word *Varank*, but only with a geographical signification. The first Mahomedan writer who mentions
the *Varank* is al-Bîrûnî (born in Chorasmia 973, +c.
1038 A.D.), an extremely learned and important
author, of whose works—as far as they are still in
existence—but a small portion has yet been published. But we learn from several more recent
writers who quote him as their authority, that he had
mentioned 'a bay of the great ocean which stretches
northwards of the Slavs and is called the Varangian
Sea (*Bahr Varank*); but *Varank* is the name of a
people who dwell on its coasts[3].' Here the name
Varank evidently denotes the Scandinavians, more
particularly the Swedes, and the 'Varangian Sea'
is clearly the Baltic, which, we observe, was called by

---

[1] "Народъ вашъ искони служилъ моимъ предкамъ: въ старыхъ лѣто-
писяхъ упоминается о Варягахъ, которые находились въ войскѣ Само-
держца Ярослава-Георгія: а Варяги были Шведы, слѣдственно его
подданные."—Карамзинъ, Исторія государства Россійскаго. Изд. четвертое.
Т. iX. стр. 214. Санктнетб. 1834.

[2] Полное собраніе русскихъ лѣтописей, изданное по высочайшему
повелѣнію археологическою коммиссіею. Т. iii. стр. 283. Санктнетб. 1841.

[3] See Frähn, Ibn Foszlan's und anderer Araber Berichte über die
Russen, p. 177.

I

the same name by the Russian chroniclers. A Persian
manuscript of Bîrûnî's 'Instruction in Astronomy'
(composed in 1029) has lately been discovered, and
we are told that in three passages of this work he
speaks of the *Varank*, and that in the map which
accompanies this manuscript they are clearly placed
on the east coast of Sweden[1]. The same name was
also mentioned by another author who is often referred to by other writers, Shîrâzî, who lived at the
end of the thirteenth and the beginning of the fourteenth century. In a more recent Turkish geography
(of the seventeenth century), entitled Jihân-numa, and
composed by Haji Khalfah, the author says as follows: 'The German Sea (*Bahr Alaman*) is called
in our geographical and astronomical books the
Varangian Sea (*Bahr Varank*). The learned Shîrâzî,
in his work called Tohfah, says, " On the coast
of it dwells a nation of tall warlike men," and by
these *Varank* he understands the Swedish people. . . .
Now this sea is called the Baltic in the languages of
the surrounding nations[2].' These instances will suffice
to show that, in Oriental terminology also, the word
Varangian, Varank, bore, from the beginning of
the eleventh century, its geographical signification
of Scandinavians, more particularly Swedes, and no
other.

As far as regards the Byzantine terminology, it is
true that the name *Varangoi* (Βάραγγοι) seems to be
used there in the sense of a certain military force.

[1] See Mémoires de l'Acad. Imp. de St. Pétersbourg, série vii. t. xxiii.
p. 368.
[2] See Frähn, l. c., p. 196.

I think, however, that was not the original meaning
of the word; as employed by the Greeks it was
also, at first, the popular[1] designation for the Scandinavians (especially the Swedes) as a nation and
not merely the name of a particular body of troops.
This is clearly indicated in Byzantine writings by
the fact that we always find the name *Varangoi*
co-ordinate with names of other nations. Thus,
·for instance, we frequently find 'Franks and Varangians' mentioned together[2]. In a passage of
Georgius Cedrenus[3] the Varangians are mentioned
in opposition to the *Romaioi*, i. e. the native Greeks,
as he says, 'the soldiers who kept watch in the
palace, both Romaioi and Varangians;' and he (or a
copyist) adds that the latter are 'a Celtic (!) nation.'
The learned and literary princess Anna Comnena
speaks of 'the Varangians from Thule,' which she
further explains as 'the axe-bearing barbarians[4];'
these she opposes first to a division of the native army

---

[1] Comp. Joh. Scylitzes, p. 808 (= 644 in the Bonn edition), Βαράγγους
αὐτοὺς ἡ κοινὴ ὀνομάζει διάλεκτος.

[2] e. g. Georg. Cedrenus, p. 787 (under the date of 1050 A.D.), τὰ συμ-
μαχικὰ πάντα, Φράγγους φημὶ καὶ Βαράγγους; id., p. 789 (1052 A.D.),
Φράγγους καὶ Βαράγγους; Joh. Scylitzes, p. 823 (under the date of 1068
A.D.), ὁ δὲ βασιλεὺς στρατὸν ἐπαγόμενος ἔκ τε Μακεδόνων καὶ Βουλγάρων
καὶ Καππαδοκῶν καὶ Οὔζων καὶ τῶν ἄλλων παρατυχόντων ἐθνικῶν πρὸς δὲ
καὶ Φράγγων καὶ Βαράγγων; id., p. 858 (1078 A.D.), μετὰ Βαράγγων καὶ
Φράγγων πλήθους πολλοῦ.

[3] P. 792 (under the date of 1056 A.D.), οἱ φυλάσσοντες ἐν τῷ παλατίῳ
στρατιῶται, Ῥωμαῖοί τε καὶ Βάραγγοι (γένος δὲ Κελτικὸν οἱ Βάραγγοι μισθο-
φοροῦντες Ῥωμαίοις).

[4] Anna Comnena, p. 62 (under the date of 1081 A.D.), τοὺς ἐκ τῆς Θούλης
Βαράγγους (τούτους δὴ λέγω τοὺς πελεκυφόρους βαρβάρους). Thule in Pro-
copius and (from his example) in mediæval Greek authors signifies the
Scandinavian peninsula, Sweden and Norway; see Cronholm, Wäringarna,

and then to the *Nemitzoi,* 'who also,' she says, 'are a barbarous nation[1].'

Kunik has also lately discovered, in the chronicle of the South-Italian convent of the Monte Cassino, written by Leo Ostiensis, the same name in the Italianised form *Guarani* or *Gualani,* and there the name is evidently employed as the name of a nation (viz. Swedes); thus 'Dani, Russi et Gualani' are mentioned (under the date of 1009) as Greek auxiliary troops who had been sent to Apulia and Calabria[2]. An Old Norse Saga finally gives testimony in the same direction. It is said in Harald Hardrada's Saga (ch. 3) that there were in Constantinople 'a great many Northmen, whom they there call Varangians[3].'

In a Russian work on the Varangians by Professor Vasilievski, which unfortunately is not accessible to me, the author is said to have proved that some Byzantines in the eleventh century used the two names *Varangoi* and *Rhos* as synonymes; and in some Greek documents lately discovered the two names form one compound word, *Varangoi-Rhos* or *Rhos-Varangoi*[4].

---

p. 35 ff. Lund, 1832, and Werlauff in Det Kgl. Danske Videnskabernes Selskabs hist. og philos. Afhandlinger, vol. vii. p. 90 ff. 1845, 4to.

[1] Ibid., τοὺς Νεμίτζους (ἔθνος δὲ καὶ τοῦτο βαρβαρικὸν καὶ τῇ βασιλείᾳ Ῥωμαίων δουλεῦον ἀνέκαθεν). The *Nemitzoi* are evidently the Germans, whom the Slavs call *Němci*. Comp. Constantine Porphyrogen. De cerimoniis aulae Byz. ii. p. 398 . . . εἰς τὸν ῥῆγα Σαξωνίας [i. e. Saxonia], εἰς τὸν ῥῆγα Βαΐούρη [i. e. Bavaria] (ἔστιν δὲ αὕτη ἡ χώρα οἱ λεγόμενοι Νεμίτζιοι).

[2] See Mémoires de l'Acad. Imp. de St. Pétb., vii. série, tome xxiii. p. 376 ff.

[3] 'Þar var mikill fjöldi Norðmanna, er þeir kalla Væringja;' Fornmanna Sögur, vol. vi. p. 135. Copenhagen, 1831.

[4] Mém. de l'Acad., Imp. l. c., pp. 378 f. 409.

Here the word can only have been used to signify a nation, and the same or nearly the same nation as that which the Greeks had previously known under the name of *Rhos*. The compound words *Varangoi-Rhos* or *Rhos-Varangoi* must then signify as much as 'Swedish Northmen' or 'Scandinavian Swedes.'

From the proofs I have already produced I think it is clear that not only did the Greeks use the word *Varangoi* as the name of a nation (Scandinavians, Swedes), but even that this was its original and most ancient signification among them. It was only afterwards when the visits of the Scandinavians to Constantinople had become rarer, and when the body-guard which they had formed was recruited more and more from other nations, that the name was simply used as the name of a military body, armed with the same weapons, and holding the same peculiar position among the Imperial guards as once did the Scandinavians. This is a change in the signification of a word to which it is easy to find parallels, whereas the employment of a word which first was used to signify body-guards to designate a nation of which this guard was chiefly composed, is certainly unexampled. I need only to remind you of the 'Swiss guards' of the French sovereigns and of the Pope at the present day, who continue to bear that name, though they have long ago ceased to consist exclusively of Swiss. The word *Zouave* also was at first the name of a single Arab tribe which levied the first troops of that particular description, but now has come to signify all sorts of troops wearing uniforms similar to those of the original Zouaves.

When we consult Scandinavian authorities we find
this peculiarity, that though the Old Norse word *Væringjar* (in the singular *Væringr* or *Væringi*) is true
Norse, yet in signification it is half foreign, since it
only signifies the Scandinavian body-guards in the
service of the Greek emperor, and has no reference to
Scandinavians in general nor to any other foreign
troops at Constantinople : thus, for instance, in Hakon
Herdibreid's Saga, chap. 21 [1], the *Væringjar* are distinctly opposed to the Franks and Flemish, whose
position in the Greek army was, however, about the
same. The word cannot have obtained this sign-
tion in the Scandinavian lands, it must have been
carried back thither by Scandinavians who had been
in Constantinople. It is quite a solitary case when
we find the word *Væringjar* in one Saga signifying
Scandinavians or Northmen in general. This is the
case in the comparatively modern Thidrek's Saga
(from c. 1250 A.D.), and as several proofs occur in the
same Saga that the author had been in Russia, or had
relations there at least, inasmuch as he appears to
be well acquainted with several localities there, it is
probable that the peculiar employment of the word
Væringjar in this Saga is an imitation of the Russian
signification of the word *Variag*', whether the author
wished to display his learning or found its use in this
sense very practical [2]. This signification of the word is
otherwise unknown in the North.

[1] Heimskringla eller Norges Kongesagaer udg. ved C. R. Unger,
p. 776. Christiania, 1868 (= Fornmanna Sögur, vol. v. p. 137. Copenhagen, 1830).

[2] Comp. G. Storm, Sagnkredsene om Karl den Store og Didrik af
Bern hos de nordiske Folk, p. 91 ff. Christiania, 1874.

When we review the evidence here produced, it seems to me unquestionable that *Varangian* was always, among the eastern nations, a geographical or national title, and that it signified the inhabitants of Scandinavia, principally the Swedes. If that be the case, there can be no doubt that the Greeks received this name from Russia. Not only had the Scandinavians been known in Russia long before the Greeks made acquaintance with them, but it was even the Russ who first introduced them in Constantinople, and the Scandinavians who afterward repaired to Greece mostly travelled through Russia on their way thither. For this very reason it seems to me absurd to suppose that the word had been coined in Constantinople and afterwards taken thence to Russia. Whether the Arabs, in their turn, received this word from the Greeks or directly from Russia, must be left undecided.

When we reflect, on the other hand, that the name is incontestably Scandinavian in its root, yet that it presents itself in Old Norse literature as a half-foreign word, only one explanation seems possible to me, an explanation which at the same time clears up all philological and historical difficulties. That is to suppose that the word took its rise among the Scandinavians who in former times settled in Russia, that is to say, among that tribe to which the Slavs applied the name *Russ*, and that it is a designation given by them to their countrymen west of the Baltic, or, at any rate, to those of them whom the brisk connection between ancient Russia and Scandinavia took over there. If this supposition be correct, we gain, in this purely Scandinavian name, a new proof of the Scandinavian nationality of the Russ.

The form which is the basis of the Russian form *Variag'*, the Greek form *Varangos*, and the Arabic form *Varank*, seems to be *Väring-*, without the change of the *ä* to *æ* which we meet with in the Old Norse form *Væringi*. As to the origin of this word, it must, at any rate, be derived from a basis *vär-*. The Old Norse really possesses several words of this same form; but among them there is certainly one only which in this case is satisfactory, namely, the same which has previously been referred to (see above, p. 111). Only, I think that the interpretation of the word *Varangian*, which from this view has been hitherto generally accepted, is not correct.

In different Teutonic languages we find a word the most ancient form of which is *värä* (Old Norse *vär-ar*, A.S. *wär*, Old High German *wära*, &c.). The signification of this word is (1) truth, faith, faithfulness; (2) (=mediæval Latin *treuga*) pledge, plighted faith, truce, peace; (3) (with reference to that person who receives the *värä* of another) security, safeguard, protection[1]. In Old Norse the word *vár* is used in the singular as the name of a goddess of faith[2]; the plural *várar* signifies a pledge, plighted faith, especially between man and wife, sometimes between personal foes[3], but never a military oath. Words akin to *várar* are in Old Norse the adjective *værr*,

---

[1] Comp. Müllenhoff in Zeitschrift für deutsches Alterthum, vol. xvi. (N. F. iv.) 1873, p. 149.

[2] Comp. Bugge, Sæmundar Edda, p. 128. Christiania, 1867.

[3] Sigrdrífumál 23 and 35, in Sæmundar Edda.

'peaceful, safe; snug, comfortable; tranquil, easy;' and the substantives *væri*, 'abode, shelter,' and *væra*, 'snugness, warmth; a rest, shelter[1].' A derivative from the same basis is the Old Norse *væringr* or *væringi*. If we review the just mentioned words, it must certainly be considered highly improbable that this word should have any especial reference to personal military service. It can scarcely signify anything but a person who finds shelter and safety somewhere[2]. From this view it may be compared with the Anglo-Saxon word *wærgenga*, which in an old glossary is interpreted 'advena,' a foreigner, but the proper signification of which is doubtless the same; in the Langobardian laws we find the corresponding word in the form *waregang*, with just the same meaning[3]. The name *Varangian* consequently signifies at first nearly as much as a denizen or a

---

[1] These words have nothing to do with the Old Norse *vera, vesa*, 'to be,' Gothic *visan*, as may be seen from the Old Norse words *úværr*, 'restless, fierce, uncomfortable' (modern Norwegian *uvær, ovær*, 'restless, uneasy, displeased'), *úværi*, 'uneasiness,' which evidently correspond to the Gothic *unvērjan*, 'to be displeased,' and *unvērei*, 'indignation;' but these Gothic words (together with *tuzvērjan*, 'to doubt') are unquestionably derived from *vēra*, which would be the Gothic form of the original *vārā*.

[2] In a verse in Egil's Saga we find the poetical compound *fold-væringi*, 'earth-dweller, i.e. the snake' (see Vigfusson, Icelandic Dictionary). The literal meaning may have been 'he who is sheltered in the earth.'

[3] 'Omnes waregang qui de exteras fines in regni nostri finibus advenerint, seque sub scuto potestatis nostrae subdederint, legibus nostris Langobardorum vivere debeant,' &c. Edictus Rothari, c. 367. In Mémoires de l'Acad. Imp. de St. Pétersb., vii. série, tome xxiii. pp. 249 ff., 372 ff., 421, Kunik has already compared these words with the Old Norse *væringi*, attempting to assign to all of them the signification of a sworn attendant; but, with all due respect to this admirable scholar, I cannot but consider this interpretation totally wrong.

metoecus; such was undoubtedly the very con-
dition of the Scandinavians who came over to Russia,
while the mastery of the country belonged to a
kindred Scandinavian tribe.

This name, which was consequently at first the 'Russian' denomination of the Scandinavians who came
over to Russia, according to their politico-social position there, was adopted by the Slavs in Russia as the
name of those people according to their nationality, and
it was extended also to denote the inhabitants of the
Scandinavian motherlands west of the Baltic, especially
Sweden. With this signification it was transmitted
to the other eastern nations, among whom we find
the word in use, and it thus gradually supplanted the
more ancient name applied to the Scandinavians in
the East, *Russ*, at the same time as this name changed
its original signification. These two names, Russ and
Varangian, far from having been synonymous, must
once, on the contrary, have been used in opposition to
each other. The relationship between them must have
been about the same as between a 'Yankee' and
an Englishman, or, among the Spaniards in America,
between a Creole (*criollo*) and a 'Chapeton' or a 'Ga-
chupin,' as they call a Spaniard from Europe. The
distinction, however, was gradually forgotten, especially as the ancient Russ lost by degrees their primitive nationality and became Slavonicised. Therefore,
according to the signification of the word in his time,
Nestor may very well have defined the primitive
Russ as a clan of the Varangians in one part of his
history, and in another have drawn a distinction
between the two names. In Scandinavia itself the

word *Varangian* was of course unknown in its eastern
signification; in more recent times it was taken there
again by Scandinavians who had resided in Constantinople, where the 'Russ' and the 'Varangians' met
and associated with each other, and where the word
had been handed down to them by tradition; in
this manner it acquired in Scandinavia that restricted signification in which we find it used in the
Old Norse Sagas.

Several questions still remain concerning the existence of the Scandinavian element in Russia. In the
first place, How long did the primitive Russ, the ruling
race in Kiev, maintain their Scandinavian nationality?
When this tribe first obtained dominion over the Slavs,
it cannot, comparatively speaking, have been very
numerous; besides the princely leaders it consisted
chiefly of warriors; still, though we learn nothing
directly about it, there can be no doubt that, like
other hosts of Northmen[1], the Russ were accompanied
by women. We know, for instance, that Rurik's son
Igor was married to one of his country-women,
named Olga (Helga), who was born in Pleskov.
Yet even if this be so, still many of these emigrants
certainly soon began to intermarry with the native
Slavonic women. Under these circumstances it seems
all the less possible that the descendants of the
original settlers, living amidst a far more numerous
Slavonic population, could have preserved their
Scandinavian nationality for more than the first three
or four generations. So far as the reigning family
is concerned, we find that Igor's son (born 942) bore

---

[1] Comp. J. Steenstrup, Indledning i Normannertiden, p. 270 ff.

the purely Slavonic name Sviatoslav; and from his
time Slavonic names, with but few exceptions, were
exclusively used in the reigning family. When Sviatoslav's son Vladimir (who died 1015) officially introduced Christianity into Russia in 988, he made the
Slavonic language the language of the Church, and
there is no doubt he at that time considered himself
in all respects a Slav, though he probably was still acquainted with the language of his forefathers. In the
time of his son and successor Yaroslav (+ 1054) the
fragile traditional ties which still bound the Russian
princes to the Scandinavian nationality were completely severed.

Though about the year 1000 the reigning house
in Kiev may be considered essentially Slavonicised,
it does not necessarily follow that by this time the
Scandinavian element had entirely disappeared from
Russia. There is much to indicate that the Russian
race was continually recruited by Varangian immigrants from the Scandinavian lands, who came, not
merely to serve for some time at the Russian court
or in the Russian army, but also to settle perma-
nently in Russia. According to the German writer
Thietmar, the population in Kiev even in the year
1018 consisted 'chiefly of Danes[1],' whereby he certainly does not mean exclusively Danes in the stricter

---

[1] 'In magna hac civitate (*Kitava*, i.e. Kiev), que istius regni caput est,
plus quam quadringente (quadraginta?) habentur ecclesiae et mercatus 8,
populi autem ignota manus, quae sicut omnis haec provincia ex fugiti-
vorum robore servorum huc undique confluencium, et *maxime ex velocibus
Danis*, multum se nocentibus Pecinegis hactenus resistebat et alios vin-
cebat.' Thietmari Chronicon, in Pertz, Monumenta Germ. hist., Script.,
vol. iii. p. 871.

sense of the word, but Scandinavians in general, in the sense in which this name was used in England at that time. From this and other evidence we seem entitled to conclude that the Scandinavian element was largely represented at Kiev even at the beginning of the eleventh century. But about this period the stream of reinforcements from the North ceases; for the abnormal conditions which had given the impulse to the Northmen's expeditions had long since ceased to exist. The complete establishment of Christianity had given an entirely new aspect to social life in the North, and the internal state of the Scandinavian countries claimed all the energies of the inhabitants. With about the year 1030 the Viking period is therefore considered to be at an end, and, in accordance with this, the Varangians are mentioned for the last time as subsidiaries in the Russian army in 1043 [1]. The few Scandinavians who were to be found at that time in Russia proper (i. e. Kiev) were left to their fate, which it is not difficult to imagine.

The state of affairs was, however, different in Novgorod and its district. Having been abandoned by the Russian clan, it had maintained for some considerable time a fairly independent position as the rival of Kiev, and attained to considerable importance by means of its flourishing trade, to which its favourable situation and easy communication with the sea through Lake Ladoga greatly contributed. There the Scandinavian element was still more largely repre-

[1] Geo. Cedrenus, p. 551; comp. Muralt, Chronographie Byzantine, p. 627, and Kunik in Mémoires de l'Acad. Imp. de St. Pétersb., vii. série, tome xxiii. p. 30 ff.

sented than in Kiev, as many Varangians, Scandinavians from Sweden, particularly from Gothland,
repaired thither for the sake of trade. How large
this Scandinavian element was, may be guessed from
Nestor's statement that Novgorod was a Varangian
town ;' and we learn from other sources that the Goth-
landers had a large guildhall there in the twelfth
century, and that there was a Varangian church
there, &c. But from the thirteenth and fourteenth
centuries the Scandinavians were forced to give way
to the Germans, and the lucrative Novgorod trade
passed into the hands of the German Hanse Towns.

In conclusion, the question is, What influence after
all has the Scandinavian element had upon the
native element in Russia, and what traces has it left
of its presence in former times? One thing is certain :
if we could analyse the blood which flows in the
veins of the ruling race of modern Russia, we should
scarcely discover in it a drop derived from a Scandinavian source. While in this respect the Finnish
tribes which once inhabited so large a portion of
the Russian empire may have exercised a somewhat
important influence, the number of Scandinavians
there was comparatively so small, that in physical
respects they could hardly have had any permanent
influence.

That in manners and customs, in social life and
political institutions in Russia, traces of Scandinavian
influence were long to be found, is undoubted. But
how many or how few these traces were is an extremely difficult question. To answer it would
necessitate much preliminary research, which indeed

ought to be undertaken, according to the modern principles of science, but which at present has not been attempted.

More marked and distinct are the effects produced on the Russian tongue by the influence of a Scandinavian language. And yet here too close examination of this question presents considerable difficulties. On one hand, we may easily be misled in this respect by resemblances which are due to the original affinity between the Slavonic and the Teutonic languages (the Slav. *grad'*, in Russian *gorod'*, a town, for instance, is a genuine Slavonic word, akin to the Old Norse *garðr*, &c.). On the other hand, we shall perceive that not only the Russian, but also the other Slavonic languages, contain a great many words which are doubtless of Teutonic origin[1]; but we shall also observe that these words are by no means homogeneous, and that they belong to different strata of language. Thus there are many words common, more or less, to all the Slavonic languages, which must have been adopted from the language of the Goths, when the Slavs still dwelt together east of the Vistula: for instance, Slav. *st'klo* (стькло), glass, from the Gothic *stikls*, a goblet; Slav. *userg'* (оусерагъ), *useręz'* (оусераѕъ), an earring, from the Gothic *ausa-hrings*, &c. A great many other words have been borrowed from the German, partly in modern, partly in earlier times.

When we have carefully separated these several

---

[1] Comp. Miklosich, Die Fremdwörter in den Slavischen Sprachen, in Denkschriften der phil.-hist. Classe der kais. Akademie, vol. xv. Wien. 1867.

strata of Teutonic words, there will remain some
which only occur in Russian, and not in the other
Slavonic languages; these in form also betray a
Scandinavian origin. In these words we are entitled
to see memorials of the Scandinavian element which
once played so important a part in the history of
Russia. The greater portion of these words are only
to be found in ancient Russian documents, inasmuch
as they indicate things and ideas which are now out
of date. Other words are preserved only in certain
dialects; but unfortunately the Russian dialects have
not as yet been thoroughly investigated, and it is
therefore impossible · for me to offer an exhaustive
list of such words [1]. The words of that kind which
I have noticed, and which I unhesitatingly affirm are
of Scandinavian origin, are the following :—

Old Russian *ask'*, *yask'* (аскъ, яскъ), a box, modern
Russian *yashchik'* (ящикъ), = Old Norse *ask-r*, Old
Swedish *ask-er*, Modern Swedish *ask*.

Old Russian *grid'* (гридь), a body-guard, attendant (of the ancient Russian princes), = Old Norse
grið, a domicile, home, with the notion of service
(*griðmaðr*, a servant, lodger).

Russian dial. *kerb'* (кербь), a bundle of flax, = Old
Norse *kerf*, *kjarf*, Swedish *kärfve*, a bundle.

Russian *knut'* (кнутъ), a whip, scourge, = Old Norse
knut-r, Old Swedish *knut-er*, a knot.

---

[1] Words of Scandinavian origin in Russian dialects (Слова областнаго
словаря сходныя съ скандинавскими) have been collected by Grot in his
Филологическія разысканія, pp. 430–442, St. Petersb., 1873; but I think
that only a very small portion of his list can be admitted by a more
severe criticism.

Russian *lar'* (ларь), a chest, = Old Swedish *lar,* modern *lår.*

(Russian *lava* (лава), a bench, couch, = Swedish *lafve?*).

Old Russian *luda* (луда), a kind of dress, a cloak, = Old Norse *loði,* a fur-cloak; *lóð,* the shagginess of cloth.

(Russian dialect (Arkhangelsk) *riuzha, riuza* (рюжа, рюза), a bow-net, weel, = Swedish *rysja,* id., which has also given the Finnish *rysä*).

Russian dialect *skiba* (скиба), a slice of bread, = Swedish *skifva,* id.

Old Russian *stiag'* (стягъ), · a banner, in modern dialects (No·gorod, Pskov) a pole, = Old Swedish *stang,* Old Norse *stöng,* a pole, a banner (the Russian sound *ia, ya,* corresponds to original *en* or *an*).

Russian *stul'* (стулъ), a chair, perhaps = Old Norse *stóll,* Swedish *stol* (rather than = German *stuhl,* which should probably in Russian have received the form *shtul'*).

Old Russian *sud'* (судъ), name of Bosporus, = Old Norse and Swedish *sund,* a sound, straits.

Old Russian *shucka* (шнека), a kind of ship, = Old Norse *snekkja,* id.; the Old French *esneque,* mediæval Latin *isnecchia,* must also have been borrowed from the Northmen.

Old Russian *tïun', tivun'* (тіунъ, тивунъ), a steward, manager (always a serf), = Old Norse *þjónn,* a servant, attendant; the Old Swedish form would be *þiun.* The Russian *tïun'* corresponds in its signification to what is commonly called in Old Norse *bryti*; but the word *þjónn* seems to have been used sometimes in a similar special signification ; comp. the Norwegian Old Gulathings-law, ch. 198, where *þjónn* and *bryti* are mentioned together as the chief servants.

Old Russian *yabednik'* (ябедникъ), an officer in ancient Novgorod ; comp. Old Norse *embætti*, Old Swedish *ambiti*, an office (?).

Russian *yakor'* (якорь), an anchor, = Swedish *ankare* (Old Norse *akkeri*).

Though this list does not pretend to be exhaustive, we can say with certainty that the number of these words is not very large ; yet they contribute to complete the picture I have tried to sketch in these Lectures.

We have seen that, according to the old Russian tradition, which is unanimously corroborated by abundance of other evidence of different kind, the first organisation of the Russian state was due to Scandinavians, *Russ* being the name by which, in ancient times, the Northmen were designated among the eastern nations ; no serious criticism will ever be able to refute this fact. It is the Northmen who laid the foundation on which the native Slavs have raised a colossal superstructure, and the insignificant germ planted by them has developed into one of the greatest empires the world has ever seen.

ÁPPENDIX.

OLD RUSSIAN PROPER NAMES.

(Compare pp. 67-73.)

LIST OF ABBREVIATIONS.

Dipl. S. = Diplomatarium Suecanum. Holmiae, 1829, ss., 4to.

Dyb. fol. = Sverikes Runurkunder granskade och utgifne af Rich. Dybeck. Stockholm, 1860-76, fol. Vol. i. Upland (U.). Vol. ii. Stock-holmslän (St.).

Dyb. 8vo. = Svenska Runurkunder, utgifne af Rich. Dybeck. Stockholm, 1855-57, 8vo.

Förstemann = E. Förstemann, Altdeutsches Namenbuch. Vol. i. Per-sonennamen. Nordhausen, 1855, ss., 4to.

L. = Runurkunder, utgifne af Joh. G. Liljegren. Stockholm, 1833, 8vo.

Steph. = The Old Northern Runic Monuments of Scandinavia and England, collected and deciphered by George Stephens. Vol. i-ii. London and Köbenhavn, 1866-68, fol.

O. N. = Old Norse.

The date under which each name occurs is added in parenthesis.

Adulb' (945) = O. N. *Auðulfr*. *AUÞULFR* L. 70 (= Dyb. fol. U. 129). *Adulphus*, Dipl. S. iii. pp. 99, 251, 271 (Upland). Compare A.S. *Eádwulf*, Old German *Audulf*, Förstemann, p. 180.

Adun' (945) = O. N *Auðunn*. *AUÞ.N*, L. 588 (= Dyb. fol. St. 171). *UÞUN* L. 879 (Södermanland). *AUÞIN* L. 1355 (W. Gotland). *Ødinnus*, Dipl. S. iii. p. 91. Compare A.S. *Eádwine*, O. Germ. *Audowin*, Förstemann, p. 179.

Aktevu (912) = O. N. *Angantýr* (A.S. *Ongenþeów*)?

Akun' (945), **Yakun'** (1024 and often) = O. N. *Hákun(n)*. *HAKUN* occurs extremely often in Swedish Runic inscrip-

K 2

tions, for instance L. 312 (= Dyb. fol. U. 1), 83 (= ib. 134), 601 (= ib. St. 247), &c. *AKUN*, L. 572 (Upl.). *Hacun*, Danish earl (Sax. Chron.).

Aldan' (945) = O. N. *Halfdanr*. One of the most common names in Swedish Runic inscriptions, written *HALFTAN*, *HALTAN*, *ALFTAN*. *Haldanus*, Dipl. S. iii. pp. 90, 261. A.S. *Healfdene* (Beowulf; Sax. Chron.; A.D. 871, 875, 876).

Alvard' (945) = O. N. · *Hallvarðr*. *ALVARþ*, L. 1480 (= Steph. 812). *Halwardus*, Dipl. S. iii. pp. 86, 91, 93, 95, &c.

Amun'd' (945) = O. N. *Ámundi; AMUTI*, L. 820, 825, 835, 840 (Södermanland) ; *Amundus*, Dipl. S. iii. pp. 100, 101, (Upland) ; or = O. N. *Hámundr ; HAMUNTI*, L. 750 (= Dyb. fol. U. 115) ; *Hamundus*, Dipl. S. iii. p. 98 (Upl.) ; compare A.S. *Heahmund ;* or = O. N. *Eymundr ; AIMUNT*, L. 959, 1053 ; *EUMUNT*, L. 1220 ; *UMUT*, L. 1186.

Apub'ksar', Apubkar', Pub'ksar', Pupsar' (945), a corrupt name in which may be concealed the O. N. *Óspakr ; USBAKA*, L. 943 ; *OSBAKR*, L. 1223.

Ar'fast' (945) = O. N. *Arnfastr*, particularly used in Sweden and Denmark. *ARNFASTR*, L. 33, 1050. *AR-FASTR*, L. 86 (Upland). · *Aruastus*, Dipl. S. iii. p. 89 (Upl.). *Arnfastus*, Saxo, p. 578.

Askold' see **Oskold'**.

Asmud' (tutor of Igor's son Sviatoslav ; c. 945) = O. N. *Ásmundr*. Extremely common in Swedish Runic inscriptions, and indeed in all Scandinavian countries. A.S. · *Osmund*, O. Germ. *Ansemund*, Förstemann, p. 109.

Bern' (945) = O. N. *Björn*. One of the most common names everywhere in Scandinavia ; in Runic inscriptions *BIARN, BIORN, BIURN, BIRN*, &c., in Latin documents *Bero*. A.S. *Beorn*, O. Germ. *Bero*, Förstemann, p. 224.

Bruny (945) = O. N. *Brúni*. Common in Swedish re-cords, very rare elsewhere in Scandinavia. *BRUNI* occurs, in Runic inscriptions from Upland, L. 685, 709, Dyb. fol. U. 85, 86 (= Steph. p. 733); from Södermanland, L. 934 (= Steph. p. 716); Dyb. 8vo. 41; from Nerike, L. 1029, 1038; from East Gotland, L. 1187. *Bruno*, Dipl. S. i. p. 188. O. Germ. *Bruni*, Förstemann, p. 283.

Budy (1018) = O.N. *Bóndi*. *BUANTI*, Dybeck, Runa 3, 11. *BUTNA* (for *BUNTA*), L. 348 (= Steph. p. 792); *Bondo*, (*Bonno*), Dipl. S. iii. pp. 95, 101, 584, 656 (Upland), &c.

Buyofast' see **Vuyofast'**.

Dir' (862) = O. N. *Dýri*. *TIURI*, L. 265, Steph. p. 633 (Upland); L. 1154 (East Gotland). *TURI*, L. 65 (Upl.); 1179 (East Gotland). *TIORI*, L. 1003. *Dyre*, Dipl. S. iii. p. 100. Compare O. Germ. *Dioro*, Förstemann, p. 337.

Egri (945) = O. N. **Hegri*. *Hegherus*, Dipl. S. iii. p. 336.

Emig' (945) = O.N. *Hemingr*. Extremely common in all the Scandinavian countries. *HIMINKR, HIMIKR, HENMIKR, HEMIK*, &c. in Runic inscriptions. Compare A.S. *Heming*.

Erlisk', Evlisk' (945), probably miswritten for *Erlik'* = O. N. *Erlingr?*

Etou' (945)?

Farlof' (907 and 912) = *Farulfr*, common in certain parts of Sweden, unknown in the rest of Scandinavia. *FARULFR* occurs in Runic inscriptions from Upland, Dyb. fol. St. 20, 248, L. 434, 439 (= Steph. p. 618), 602, 827; from Södermanland, Dyb. 8vo. 39; from East Gotland, L. 1176. *Farulphus* Dipl. S. iii. p. 90 (Upl.). &c. Compare O. Germ. *Faraulf*, *Farulf*, Förstemann, p. 400.

Fost' (912) = *Fasti*, *Fastr*. Scarcely used except in Sweden, but very common there. We find it in inscriptions from Upland, L. 151 (= Dyb. fol. U. 202), 158, 224, 261, 277, 452, 462 (= ib. St. 104), 463, 464 (= ib. 97), 573 (= ib. 187), 589 (= ib. 172), 641; from Södermanland, L. 818, 837, 949; from East Gotland, L. 1133, 1657. *Fasto* Dipl. S. iii. pp. 99, 258 (Upl.); *Fastæ* ib. ii. p. 394 (Södermanland).

Frastên' (945), **Prastên'** (945, thrice) = O.N. *Freysteinn.*
One of the most common names in Swedish records (in
runes *FRAUSTAIN, FRAISTAIN, FRUSTIN, FRYSTEN,*
&c.).

Frelaf' or **Frelav'** (912) = O. N. *Friðleifr, Frilleifr.*
Compare O. Germ. *Friduleib,* Förstemann, p. 427.

Frudi (945) = O. N. *Fróði. FRUþA* (accus.), L. 1096
(East Gotland). *Frodho* Dipl. S. iv. p. 16. Compare A.S.
Fróda (Beowulf), O. Germ. *Frodo,* Förstemann, p. 432.

Frutan (945)?

Fur'stên' (945) probably = O. N. *þorsteinn,* an extremely
common name. As to f = þ, compare Russian *Feodor'* =
Greek Θεόδωρος.

Gomol' (945) = O. N. *Gamall;* frequent in Sweden,
especially in Upland (for instance *KAMAL,* L. 166, 210, 371,
475, 558, 651, 781), rare in Norway, unknown in this form
in Iceland (whereas *Gamli* occurs there).

Grim' (945) = O. N. *Grímr;* very common in the whole
of Scandinavia.

Gudy (912 and 945) = Runic *KUþI,* L. 362 (Upland),
1235, which may represent either *Góði,* from *góðr,* good
(compare *Gothe,* Dipl. S. iii. p. 88, and A.S. *Goda,* Sax.
Chron., A.D. 988, O. Germ. *Godo,* Förstemann, p. 529), or
Guði = Icelandic *goði,* a priest.

Giunar' (945) = O. N. *Gunnarr.* Extremely frequent, also
in Sweden. A.S. *Gúðhere,* O. Germ. *Gundachar,* Förstemann,
p. 562.

Gunastr' (945) = O. N. *Gunnfastr;* a name peculiar to
Sweden, which more frequently occurs in the form *Guð-
fastr* (Runic *KUþFASTR*).

Igel'd' In'gel'd' (912 and 945)=O.N. *Ingjaldr. IN-
KIALTR, IKIALTR* in Runic inscriptions, *Ingeldus* in Latin
documents. A.S. *Ingeld* (Beowulf), O. Germ. *Ingild,* Förstemann, p. 784.

Igor' (+945), Ἴγγωρ, Ἴγγορ in Greek documents, *Inger* in Liudprand, = O. N. *Ingvarr.* Very common in Sweden, particularly in Upland and Södermanland. Besides the inscriptions mentioned above (p. 81 f.) we have *INKVAR*, L. 436 (= Dyb. fol. St. 128), 484 (= ib. 135), 601 (= ib. 247), 605, 650 (= ib. 23), 927 (Södermanl.), &c. *IKVAR*, L. 437 (= Dyb. fol. St. 127), 562 (= ib. 236), 1106 (East Gotland). *INGVAR*, Dyb. fol. St. 81 (= L. 423). *Inguarus* is extremely frequent in Dipl. S. Compare O. Germ. *Inguheri*, Förstemann, p. 785.

In'gel'd' see Igel'd'.

Ingivlad' (945) = O. N. *Ingivaldr.* A name peculiar to Sweden. *INKIVALTR* for instance L. 83, 481 (= Steph. p. 788). *Ingiualdus, Ingeualdus* very often in diplomata.

Iskusev', Iskusevi (945)?

Istr' (945) = *ISTRUR*, L. 753 (= Dyb. fol. U. 120)? or = O. N. *Eistr*, in Runic inscriptions *AIST(R)*, *IST(R)*?

Ivor' (945, 1109, &c.) = O. N *Ivarr*, a common Scandinavian name.

Kanitsar' (*Kanimar*? 945)?

Karl' (907) = O. N. *Karl.* One of the most frequent names in Sweden. Compare O. Germ. *Carl*, Förstemann, p. 303.

Karly (912) = O. N. *Karli. 'KARLI*, L. 1557 (East Gotland). Just as in O. N. we find the forms *Karl* and *Karli* applied indiscriminately to the same person, it seems to be the same man that is called in 907 *Karl'* and in 912 *Karly.*

Karn' (912) = *Karni*, whence the accusative case *KARNA*, L. 1188 (East Gotland)? Elsewhere unknown.

Karshev' (945) = O. N. *Karlsefni?* or = *KARSI*, L. 506, 515 (Upland)?

Kary (945) = O. N. *Kári*, frequent in all the Scandinavian countries.

Klek' (945) = *Klakki* (*KLAKI*, L. 936, 1278, 1400)?
Some manuscripts have *Vlekov'* or *Slekov'* instead of *Klekov'*.

K ɔl' (945) = O. N. *Kollr*, which rather frequently occurs
in Sweden, for instance, *Collo*, Dipl. S. iii. p. 101 (Upl.), *Coll*,
Saxo, p. 381.

Kuci (945) perhaps = O. N. *Kussi*, (a calf). This word,
which is often used as a surname, may undoubtedly, though
I can quote no instance of it, have been employed also as
a personal name quite as well as the synonym *Kalfr*, which
is very frequent in this use. (The name *KUSI* is perhaps
to be found in the Runic inscription Dyb. fol. St. 196 =
Dyb. 8vo. 69.)

Libi (945)?

Lidul' (912) = O.N. *Leiðulfr*? Compare *LITULF*, L. 4
(Upland)?

Liut' (975) may be = O. N. *Ljótr*, *LIUTR*, L. 274, Dyb.
fol. U. 214; but it may just as well be Slavonic (*liut'*, cruel).

Malfrid' (+ 1000) = O. N. *Malmfríðr*, *Málfríðr*.

Mony (945) = *Manni* (from *maðr*, *mann*, a man) which
does not appear to occur in the Norse-Icelandic Saga-literature, but is common in Sweden and Denmark. *Manne*, Dipl.
S. i. p. 53 (Skåne); iii. p. 92 (Upland); *Manno*, ib. i. p. 708
(Småland). Comp. A.S. *Manna*, Sax. Chron., A.D. 921, O.
Germ. *Mannus*, *Manni*, Förstemann, p. 903. It must be well
distinguished from the O.N. name *Máni* (literally the moon),
which in Slavonic could not become *Mony* but only *Many*.
In Runic inscriptions we often find *MANI* (e.g. from Upland
L. 491, 616, 617, from Södermanland L. 860, 901), which
doubtless mostly represents *Manni*, double letters being un-
known in Runic writing.

Mutur' or **Mutor'** (945) = O.N. *Móðþórr?* or *Munþórr?*
neither of these names occur in the records, but may very
well be supposed.

Oleb' or **Uleb'** (945) = O. N. *Óleifr*, afterwards *Ólafr*.

One of the most common names in all Scandinavia. The Slavonic *ě* presupposes the O. N. diphthong *ei* (or *ai*), and in Swedish Runic inscriptions we really always find it written *OLAIFR* or *ULAIFR*. A.S. *Anláf.*

Ol'ga (the wife of Igor, + 969), Ἔλγα in Greek authors = O. N. *Helga.*

Ol'g', Oleg' (+ 913) = O.N. *Helgi* (comp. A.S. *Hálga*). Both this name and the preceding one are very frequent in all parts of the Scandinavian countries. They must originally have been adopted by the Slavs in the forms *Yelg', Yelga* (compare the Greek Ἔλγα); afterwards *ye* was changed into *o* according to a phonetic law peculiar to Russian; compare Russian *olén'* = O. Slav. *yelen'*, a deer; Russ. *odín'* = O. Slav. *yedin'*, one; O. Russ. *olïad'*, a galley, from the Greek χελάνδιον.

Ol'ma = O. N. *Holmi*, a frequent name in Sweden (L. 513, 522, 554, 628, 657, 1038, 1236)?

Oskold' or Askold' (862) = O.N. *Höskuldr* (in Irish records *Ascall*, comp. The War of the Gaedhil with the Gaill, ed. by J. H. Todd, p. 233. London, 1867).

Prastên' see Frastên'.

Roald' see Ruald'.

Rognêd' (daughter of Rogvolod', + 1000) = O. N. *Ragnheiðr, Ragneiðr*. Compare O. Germ. *Reckinheid*, Förstemann, p. 1018.

Rogvolod' ('had come from beyond the sea;' prince of Polotsk; 980) = O. N. *Ragnvaldr. RAHNVALTR*, L. 397 (= Dyb. fol. St. 46); *RAKNVALT*, L. 436, 437 (= ib. 127, 128); *Ragualdus*, Dipl. S. iii. p. 87, 260 (Upl.), &c.

Ruald' (912 and 945), Roald' (A. 945) = O. N. *Hróaldr. HRUALTR*, Dyb. 8vo. 2. *Hroald* Danish earl, Sax. Chron. A.D. 918. Comp. O. Germ. *Hrodowald*, Förstemann, p. 741.

Ruar' (912) = O.N. *Hróarr. HRUAR*, L. 1329 (West Gotland); *RUAR*, L. 1104 (East Gotland); *RUARI* (dative),

Dyb. 8vo. 46 (Södermanland). *Roarus*, Dipl. S. iii. p. 163.
Perhaps = A.S. *Hróðgár*, O. Germ. *Hrodgar*, Förstemann,
p. 727.

Rulav' (907 and 912) = O. N. *Hróðleifr*, *Hrolleifr*.
RULAIFR, L. 1550 (= Dyb. fol. Upl. 34); *RULEFR*, L. 174
(Upl.); *RULIF(R)*, L. 143, 165 (= Dyb. fol. Upl. 208), 973
(Södermanland). *Rodlevus*, Dipl. S. iii. p. 101 (Upl.). Compare
O. Germ. *Hrodleif*, Förstemann, p. 735.

Rurik', Riurik' (862) = O. N. *Hrœrekr. HRURIKR*, L. 1096
(East Gotland). *Rþrik*, Dipl. S. iii. p. 97 (Upl.); *Rþricus*,
ib. ii. pp. 8, 37, 88, 102, 105; iii. pp. 89, 94, 256, &c. A. S.
Hréðric, O. Germ. *Hrodric, Ruodrich*, Förstemann, p. 740.

Sfan'da? (945; the reading is not certain) a female
name the first element of which appears to be O. N. *Svan-*
(as in O. N. *Svanhildr, Svanlaug*, &c.).

Sfir'k', Sfir'ka (945) = *Sverkir*, a frequent name in
Sweden where several kings bore this name. In Norway
and Iceland the form *Sörkvir* had the preference.

Shibrid' (945) = O. N. *Sigfröðr* (in the Sagas always
Sigfröðr, Sigröðr). *SIKFIKUþR*, L. 126 (= Dyb. fol. Upl.
156); *SIKRITR*, L. 80 (= ib. 148, Steph. 723); *SIHFRIþR*, L.
1731. *Sigfridus*, Dipl. S. iii. pp. 99, 389. Compare O. Germ.
Sigifrid, Förstemann, p. 1091.

Shikh'bern' or **Shigobern'** (945) = *Sigbjörn*, which never
appears in O. N. book-literature, but is very common in
Swedish records. *SIKBIARN*, L. 294 (= Dyb. fol. Upl. 256),
545 (= ib. St. 214). *SIHBIARN*, L. 523, 780 (Upland).
SIKBIURN, L. 1061, 1133, &c. *Sigbernus*, Dipl. S. iii. pp.
98, 112, 541. Compare O. Germ. *Sigipero*, Förstemann,
p. 1088.

Sineus' (862) = O. N. *Signiutr (Signjótr)*, which often
occurs in Upland, but scarcely elsewhere in the North, never
in the Saga-literature. *SIKNIUTR*, L. 204, 360 (= Dyb. fol.
St. 70), 669 (= ib. Upl. 58). *SIKNIOT*, L. 500 (= ib. St.

144). *SIHNIUTR*, Steph. 620 (= L. 269). *SIHNIUTA*, L. 214 (= Dyb. fol. U. 189). *Signiatus*, Dipl. S. i. p. 530.

Sinko Borich, Isino Kobirich, Isin'ko Birich (945), a corrupt name which can hardly be restored.

Sludy (945) = *Slóði*. Frequent in Södermanland and Upland, elsewhere unknown. From Södermanland: *SLOÞI*, L. 916, 953 (= Steph. 741), 966 (= Säve in Kgl. Vitterhets, Hist. och Antiquitets Akademiens Handlingar, vol. xxvi. p. 356. Stockholm, 1869), Dyb. 8vo. 41, 83. From Upland: *SLUÞI*, L. 280, Dyb. fol. Upl. 142.

Stemid' (907 and 912) perhaps = O. N. *Steinviðr*, though no example of this name seems to be preserved; but names in *-viðr* were extremely common and numerous in Sweden.

Stengi (written *Steggi*; 945) perhaps = O. N. *Steingeirr* (*STAINKIR*, Dyb. 8vo. 40)?

Stir' (945) = O. N. *Styrr*. *STUR*, L. 162 (Upl.). *Styr*, Dipl. S. iii. p. 98 (ib.).

Stud'k', Studek' (945) = *Staðingr*, a name which is known only from Upland and East Gotland. In East Gotland occurs *STUÞIKR*, L. 1113 (= Steph. 614); in Upland *STUÞIK*, L. 128 (= Dyb. fol. Upl. 154); *STÖÞINKR*, L. 206 (= ib. 182). (*Styinge*, Dipl. S. iii. pp. 88, 89; *Stying*, ib. p. 89?)

Svôn' (945) = O. N. *Sveinn*. One of the most frequent names in Sweden, and indeed in all Scandinavian countries.

Svênald' (945 and later) = *Sveinaldr*, which often occurs in Sweden, but scarcely outside that country. *SVINALTR*, L. 469 (= Dyb. fol. St. 113). *SVAINALTI*, L. 917 (Södermanland). *SVAINALTR*, L. 1123 (East Gotland). *Suanaldus*, Dipl. S. iii. p. 95 (Upl.); *Swenaldus*, ib. iv. p. 646.

Tilon', Tiloi, or Tiroi (945), a corrupt name of very uncertain form.

Truan' (912) = O. N. (*þróandr,) *þróndr, þrándr*. *ÞO-RONTR*, L. 170 (= Dyb. fol. Upl. 205); *ÞRUNT*, L. 1176

(East Gotland). *Thronder*, Dipl. S. iii. p. 65. Compare O. Germ. *Throand*, Förstemann, p. 1198.

Truvor' (862) ⊫ O. N. *þorvarðr.* In Sweden and Denmark we sometimes find the syllable *þor-* in similar names changed into *þru-, Tru-*; compare *þRUNIUTR* for *þURNIUTR*, L. 806; *Thrugotus*, Saxo p. 596 = *þorgautr*; *Thrugillus* (Saxo p. 513, Dipl. S. ii. p. 257, Langebek, Scriptores rerum Dan. viii. 233, &c.), Swedish *Truls*, Danish *Truels* = O. N. *þorgils ;* Swedish *Truve* (Rääf, Ydre-Målet eller Folkdialekten i Ydre Härad af Öster Götland, p. 124. Örebro 1859), probably = O. N. *þorviðr.*

Tuky (1068) = O.N. *Tóki.* Frequent, especially in Sweden and Denmark.

Tulb' (945) = *þolfr*, which occurs only in Sweden and Denmark: *þULFR*, L. 1120 (East Gotland), 1416 (Skåne). (Some manuscripts have *Tuad'*, of which Miklosich in his edition of Nestor makes *Truad' ;* but this correction is unnecessary and scarcely can be right).

Tur'bern' (945) = O. N. *þorbjörn.* Extremely frequent everywhere in the North.

Tur'brid' (945) = O. N. *þorfriðr. þORFRIþ* L. 367 (= Dyb. fol. St. 2). *þURFRIþ* L. 1098 (East Gotland). In O. N. book-literature this name has the form *þórröðr* (compare *Shibrid'*).

Turd' (945) = O. N. *þórðr.*⎫
Tury (945) = O. N. *þórir.* ⎬ Both extremely frequent.

Ul'b' (945) = O.N. *Ulfr*, if this reading is the true one. The manuscripts have **Uléb'** which may be = O. N. *Óleifr* (compare *Oléb'*).

Ustin' (945) perhaps = O.N. *Eysteinn ;* but the reading of the name is not certain.

Ver'mud' (907 and 912) = O. N. *Vermundr.*

Voist' Voikov' (945), two very doubtful names.

Vuyefast' (945) perhaps = O. N. *Véfastr. VIFAST,* L.

41 (= Dyb. fol. Upl. 42), 318 (= ib. 6). *Vyfaster,* Dipl. S. ii.
p. 231, *Viuastir* ib. S. iii. p. 89. Miklosich in his edition of
Nestor gives *Buyefasf*, perhaps = *Bófastr*, compare *Bofester*,
Dipl. S. i. p. 188 ; *Bowastus,* ib. iii. p. 657.

Vuzlêv' or Vuzlêb' (945)?

Yakun' see Akun'.

Yatviag', Yavtiag' or Yastiag' (945)?

ADDITIONS.

(To pp. 52-66.)

In the Dutch Review 'Mnemosyne, Bibliotheca philologica Batava,' Nova Series, vol. iv. pars iv. pp. 378-382, Professor C. G. Cobet has lately published that passage of Constantine Porphyrogenitus in which he gives us the names of the Dnieper rapids, according to a new and exact collation of the chief MS. of this author. This MS. is written on parchment, in the eleventh or twelfth century, and is preserved in the National Library at Paris (No. 2009, 4to.). The same Library possesses also another MS. of inferior value (No. 2967 fol.), written on paper in the fifteenth century; this MS., according to Professor Cobet, is a mere copy of the other. The small specimen Prof. Cobet gives us sufficiently proves how uncritical all the previous editions of this author are, and how much a new edition is to be desired.

Among the names of the rapids there are two for which Prof. Cobet has proved that the traditional forms which we find in the printed editions are not correct. As the interpretation of these two names must be somewhat modified in consequence of this discovery—by which I could not profit before the conclusion of my manuscript—I shall venture to give here some additional remarks upon this subject.

The name of the fourth rapid (p. 57 ff.) is not in Russ Ἀειφάρ, *Aïfar*, as the printed editions have hitherto constantly given it, but according to both MSS. Ἀειφόρ, *Aïfor*

This reading gives us at once a still better interpretation than that which I propounded above (p. 63). The name now undoubtedly turns out to be a compound, of which the former part is the Old Norse particle *ei, ey, æ*, ever, while the latter part is the Old Norse adjective *forr*, forward, precipitate, violent, and not the substantive *fari*. This adjective, which is still used in Norway in the form *for* (see I. Aasen, Norsk Ordbog, p. 177. Christiania, 1873), is, in all probability, the base of the word *fors*, a waterfall, rapid, or at least a derivative from the same radical. *Eyforr, Eiforr* (in Old Swedish *Aiforr*) consequently means 'the ever violent,' 'ever rapid' ('perpetuo praeceps'), a name which is in fact still more expressive than '*Eifari*,' literally 'aye-faring,' 'going on for ever.'

The other of the names in question is that of the seventh rapid (p. 65 f.), which all editions give us in the form Στρού- βουν, *Struvun* (or *Strubun*), and such is in fact the word in the paper MS. 2967. But the original parchment MS. 2009 has most distinctly Στρούκουν, *Strukun*, which consequently must be considered to be the correct reading. If it be so, this name cannot any more, of course, be referred to the Old Norse *straumr*, a stream, but the true interpretation can be easily found. In Norse we find the words *strok* (neutr.) or *stryk* (masc.), 'a rapid current in a river, especially where it is narrow' (see Aasen, l. c., pp. 761, 762); in Swedish dialects the corresponding word, with the same signification, is found in the form *stråk* or *struk* (neutr.) (see Rietz, Ordbok öfver Svenska Allmogespråket, p. 685. Lund, 1867); Rietz gives us also a feminine word *strukk*, 'a small rapid which it is possible to ascend by rowing.' I have no doubt that the name *Strukun* represents this very word in its Swedish form *struk* (as to the vowel *u*, comp. p. 55, note 1); in this way the name most exactly agrees with the translation of Constantine, 'the small rapid,' with the corresponding Slavonic name, and with the character of the place. The termination -*un* of the form *Strukun* only remains doubtful. It can hardly be the definite article of the Scandinavian languages, which is seldom or never used in proper names. It rather looks like the Old Norse and Old Swedish termination of the dative plur. -*um*; if it be so, we may imagine that the dative form *Strukum* originally, in Russ, happened to be governed by some preposition, e.g. *at*, at, to; and thus *Strukum* might be supposed to be the name of the rapid. How it happened so is of course a mere matter of guess-work; though it may be ascribed with more probability to some error of Constantine or his authority, than to some real peculiarity in the denomination of this place. Let me add, that there may possibly be some connection between this form and the syllable *na-* in the corresponding Slavonic name *Naprezi*, *na* being a Slavonic preposition with the signification 'on' or 'at.'

I have made no remark on the name Σαμβατάς, *Sambatas*, which is said to be another name of Kiev (p. 52). Though it is not expressly stated, it can scarcely be doubted that this word, which cannot be Slavonic, gives us the 'Russian' name of that town. No satisfactory interpretation of this name has hitherto been propounded, nor can I explain it with certainty. I venture, however, to put forth the hypothesis that it might be the Old Norse *Sandbakki*, the sandbank, or *Sandbakka-áss*, the sandbank-ridge. I believe that this interpretation would suit the character of the place, but I cannot affirm it, and must leave the decision of this question to others. (Gedeonov explains the name *Sambatas* from the Hungarian *szombat*, which he translates 'a fortress,' and he employs this interpretation in support of the fantastic hypothesis that Askold and Dir were Hungarians. The Hungarian *szombat*, however, signifies nothing but 'Saturday'; it is borrowed from the Slavonic *sabota*, i.e. Sabbath.

What may have induced Gedeonov to assign to this word the fictitious signification ' a fortress,' is its frequent occurrence in names of towns and villages in Hungary; but also the names of the other days of the week are used in this manner, a circumstance which may probably be explained from the peculiar custom of calling a place from its market-day. Thus we are told that the word *szombat* exists in fourteen local names of Hungary and five of Transylvania; *szerda*, Wednesday, in nineteen names of Hungary and six of Transylvania; *péntek*, Friday, in seven names of Hungary and four of Transylvania, &c. But the days of the week are, among the Hungarians, a Christian institution; consequently their names did not yet exist in Hungarian at the period to which the name *Sambatas* belonged. Comp. C. W. Smith, Nestors Russiske Krönike, p. 352. Kjöbenhavn, 1869. Hunfalvy, in Nyelvtudományi Közlemények, vol. vi. p. 216 f. Pest, 1867. Roesler, Romänische Studien, p. 134. Leipzig, 1871.)

INDEX

www.ingramcontent.com/pod-product-compliance
Lightning Source LLC
Chambersburg PA
CBHW020552270326
41927CB00006B/808